Cook It Like A Native

Recipes & Stories From
Dade County's Colorful Past

THE VILLAGERS

Cook It Like A Native

A cookbook of time-honored favorites from The Villagers, Inc., Miami, Florida

Proceeds from the sale of this cookbook will be reinvested in the community through The Villagers, Inc., projects.

The Villagers, Inc.
P.O. Box 141843
Coral Gables, FL 33114-1843
email: info@thevillagersinc.org

STUDIO PHOTOGRAPHY BY
Lulu & Petunia Photography, Inc.
© 2008

LOCATION PHOTOGRAPHY BY
Robin Hill Photography, Inc.
© 2008

DESIGNED BY
Tom Reno Design

MANUFACTURED BY
StorterChilds Printing Co., Inc.

LIBRARY OF CONGRESS
CONTROL NUMBER: **2008939811**

ISBN:
978-0-9821981-0-0

COVER PHOTOGRAPH:
Richmond Cottage, Deering Estate at Cutler, generously underwritten by Maxine B. Wishart

Manufactured in the United States of America
First Printing: 2008
3,000 copies

THE VILLAGERS
INCORPORATED
DEDICATED TO THE RESTORATION AND PRESERVATION OF HISTORIC SITES

Looking out to Biscayne Bay from the second-floor veranda of The Barnacle, former home of pioneer Commodore Ralph Munroe.

The Villagers have helped in the restoration efforts at Venetian Pool in Coral Gables, including the hands-on project of painting the wrought iron fence in 1987.

MAJOR SPONSORS

Special thanks to our major contributors for their gracious and generous support which has made possible the beautiful cover and title page photographs.

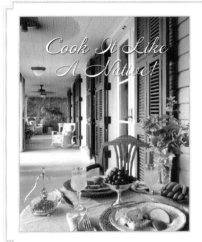

Heritage Hero

Maxine Brown Wishart

Porch of Richmond Cottage,
Deering Estate at Cutler / *Book Cover*

Preservation Patron

Arthur Hertz,
Miami Seaquarium

The Barnacle
Historic State Park / *Title Page*

We are deeply indebted to the photographers for the many hours they spent taking the spectacular photographs in this cookbook.

Location Photography: **Robin Hill Photography, Inc.**
Quilt Photography: **Lulu & Petunia Photography, Inc.**

PIONEER PARTNERS

The inclusion of photographs and histories was made possible through the generous underwriting by the following people and organizations. We are honored that such a wide variety of community support sponsored this endeavor.

MARIAH BROWN

Ms. Peggy C. Hall and Dr. Sandra Riley,
Jane Allen Petrick, Ph.D.,
The Honorable Desca DuBois, Mayor, Town of Lake Park, Florida

WILLIAM JENNINGS BRYAN

Jacqueline Norris Huggett Living Trust,
Barbara J. Lange and Lyn Parks

CHARLES DEERING

The Deering Estate Foundation, Inc.

JAMES DEERING

Vizcaya Museum and Gardens and The Vizcayans

MARJORY STONEMAN DOUGLAS

The Gardner Family Foundation, Inc.

DAVID FAIRCHILD

Raymond Jungles, Incorporated
Landscape Architect

CARL FISHER

Greenstreet Real Estate Partners, L.P.
*An investment and asset management
company operating throughout the U.S.*

DR. JAMES J. JACKSON

Dade Heritage Trust Advisors and Trustees:
Becky Roper Matkov, President/CEO; Walter A. Alvarez, Chairman;
Bertram J. "Chico" & Cindy Goldsmith; Betty S. Brody; Lisa W. Chaffin;
Peggy Groves; Ruth Jacobs; Dolly MacIntyre; Bruce C. Matheson;
Enid C. Pinkney; Amy E. Sussman, P.A.; and Mary M. Young

HUGH M. MATHESON

Baker Foundation – The Decker Family,
Kimberly and Marshall Criser, Pamela Ibargüen,
Patricia and Oscar Mederos, Maria Lourdes Solares

GEORGE MERRICK

Harry and Mary Perrin Fund, Don Slesnick II, Fund Advisor
Coral Gables Community Foundation

COMMODORE RALPH MUNROE

The Barnacle Society, Inc.

THE TRAPP FAMILY

Lisa and Victor Mendelson

TROPICAL TRAILBLAZERS

We are grateful to our sponsors whose generosity enabled us to share the beautiful photographs of some of the historic properties the Villagers have assisted in preserving over the past forty-two years.

VENETIAN POOL
Major Sponsors

Villager Presidents from 1994 – 1999
Pat Ormond, Judy Mangasarian,
Barbara Guilford, Joyce Seibert and Judy Pruitt

SPANISH MONASTERY
Table of Contents

Greenberg Traurig, P.A.

DOUGLAS ENTRANCE
Introduction To The Villagers

Claire-Frances Whitehurst

SEMINOLE THEATRE MARQUEE
Special Thanks

Joann and Roger Trombino

SIMPLE STARTS
Gatehouse at Fairchild Tropical Gardens

Anne and Dick Munday

ANIMAL CRACKERS IN MY SOUP
Original Entrance to Parrot Jungle

Lisa Wishart Chaffin, Holly Valkenaar Evans,
Joan Zellers Gache, Donna Sieger Hennessy,
Patricia Brocato Mederos, Ellen Clawson Nagel,
Lisa Sprinkle Wheeler, and Maxine Brown Wishart

EAT YOUR GREENS
"El Jardin," Carrolton School

Villager 2008-2009 "New" Members.
New members are listed on page 239.

MADE WITH LOVE
Coconut Grove Women's Club

Villager Presidents from 1999 – 2004
Victoria "Vicky" Belcher, Ellen Uguccioni, Lee Pinto,
Ann Eldredge, and Jaye Turnbull

PERFECTLY POLITE PASTA
Schoolhouse at Plymouth Congregational Church

Carmen Ortiz-Butcher, Joyce Panciera Pippo,
Lynda Botte Randolph, and Mary Martin Young

SUPPER IS SERVED
Montgomery Botanical Center

Villager Presidents from 2004 – 2009
Lisa Chaffin, Bobbi Rosenberger, Silvia Licha,
Martha Anne Collins, and Elizabeth "Liz" Juerling

BOUNTY FROM THE BAY
Lightkeeper's Cottage at Cape Florida Lighthouse

Marta N. Fernandez Trust

SASSY SIDETRACKS
Mini Train at Virginia Key Beach Park

CROWD PLEASERS
Coral Gables Congregational Church

Christina and John Butler

THE DEVIL MADE ME DO IT
Courtroom 6-1 at the Dade County Courthouse

Villager Presidents from 1982 -1994
Mary "Cookie" Thelen, Judy Zeder, Joan Bounds,
Louise Petrine, Cheryl Livesay, and Kay Gardner

Thank You

CULINARY CURATORS

Many costs are incurred when developing a cookbook. We especially thank the following individuals and organizations for allowing us to do all the other costly little things that a project like this incurs such as postage, photographer permits, the services of graphic designers, ISBN numbers, therapy sessions...

*Without your contribution we would not have
been able to produce so elegant a cookbook.*

The Allen Morris Company

The Biltmore Hotel

Archaeological and Historical Conservancy, Inc.

Civica, LLC, Architects and Urban Design,
Rolando Llanes, President

Cure & Penabad Architects

Jorge & Alina Hernandez / Jorge L. Hernandez Architect PA

Kathleen and Lamar Kauffman

MC Harry and Associates, Inc. Architects

Northern Trust

Sheila and Walter Revell

R. J. Heisenbottle Architects, P.A.

Tricia and Martin Sandler

STA Architectural Group

Fullerton Diaz Architects

QUILT KEEPERS

Since 1989 the Villagers have been creating beautiful quilts that feature a special aspect of our community, whether historical or environmental. We are very appreciative of the quilt owners for loaning their prize quilts, and especially our "Quilt Keepers" for so generously underwriting the photographs.

Ocean Waves Page 72
Photo sponsored by: Coconut Grove Bank, owned by Karin Sastre

Dade County Christmas Pine Page 73
Photo sponsored by: Norah K. Schaefer, owned by Nina Derks

El Jardin's Jewels Page 77
Photo sponsored by: Trish B. Bell, owned by Joan Bounds

House Tour Page 78
Photo sponsored by: Margaret Seroppian, owned by Victoria "Vicky" Belcher

Mariner's Compass Page 79
Photo sponsored by: Community Bank of Florida, owned by Kate LaRoche

Everglades Page 81
Photo sponsored and owned by: Cheryl Livesay

Art Deco SoBe (South Beach) Page 82
Photo sponsored by: Malinda Cleary, owned by Helen Gannon

Stiltsville Page 84
Photo sponsored by: Lynda L. Randolph, owned by Laura Kline

Stiltsville Wall Hanging Page 85
Photo sponsored and owned by: Lisa and Lynn Chaffin and Family

Destination Miami Page 86
Photo sponsored by: Frances "Dolly" MacIntyre, owned by Joann Trombino

Calle Ocho Page 87
Photo sponsored by: Joyce P. Pippo, owned by Rosemary Welton

Gifts From The Sea Page 89
Photo sponsored by: Janet Green, owned by The Mederos Family

Flor-da-lilly Page 89
Photo sponsored by: Slesnick and Associates, LLC

The Villagers hold their meetings at historic sites around Dade County, such as the Old Spanish Monastery, a 12th century structure that was dismantled and brought to the U.S. by William Randolph Hearst in 1925.

TABLE OF CONTENTS

17   SIMPLE STARTS
Appetizers and Cocktails

33   ANIMAL CRACKERS
IN MY SOUP
Soups and Chowders

53   EAT YOUR GREENS
Salads and Such

71   MADE WITH LOVE
Breads, Chutneys and Quilts

95   PERFECTLY
POLITE PASTA

109   DADE COUNTY
PIONEERS

135   SUPPER IS SERVED
Meats, Poultry and Quiche

161   BOUNTY FROM THE BAY
Seafood

181   SASSY SIDETRACKS
Vegetables and Grains

195   CROWD PLEASERS
Feeding the Multitudes

213   THE DEVIL MADE
ME DO IT
Desserts

15   INTRODUCTION
TO THE VILLAGERS
Cookbook Committee

235   SPECIAL THANKS
Cultural Contributors

*Style & Content
Consultants*

*Recipe Contributors
and Testers*

Villager Members

241   INDEX

*In 1966, a group of women banded together to help save the 1927
Coral Gables landmark, the Douglas Entrance, from demolition.
These women would become the charter members of The Villagers, Inc.*

INTRODUCTION

Since 1966, The Villagers have dedicated their time and energy to preserving the unique history of Dade County. Over the years we have used various fund-raising tools to finance historic preservation projects and scholarships. This is only our second cookbook in twenty years.

Every detail of the cookbook has been lovingly prepared by the cookbook committee. As the title suggests, Cook It Like A Native pays tribute to the rich history of our community.

Nestled in the center of the book are some of the famous (and infamous) pioneers who helped shape our community. Without their contributions, Dade County would not be what it is today.

Each of the ten chapters highlights a special restoration project that the Villagers were a part of over the last forty-two years. We were lucky enough to recruit internationally acclaimed photographer Robin Hill, who specializes in architecture and historic preservation, to bring a visual flair to these beautiful sites.

The recipes collected are an eclectic mixture of historical, family favorites, and other tried-and-true recipes. Our Made With Love chapter includes our famous breads and chutneys that are always a hit at the annual House and Garden Tours which have become our major fundraising events each year. The talented local studio of Lulu & Petunia Photography styled beautiful shots of a sampling of our quilts that have been raffled over the years.

The Villagers are known for their hospitality and have shared many recipes geared to entertaining throughout the cookbook, especially in the chapter Crowd Pleasers. With an eye on simplicity, and the belief that we should be with our guests and not in the kitchen, most of the recipes take a minimum of time and effort.

The Villagers invite you to explore our fascinating history, cook our favorites, and join us in toasting our past and our future.

The Villagers Cookbook Committee

Committee Co-Chair	*Committee Co-Chair*	Gayle Duncan
Kendra H. Brennan	Kathleen Slesnick	Penny Lambeth
	Kauffman	Maxine B. Wishart
Sponsor/Contribution Chair		Carmen Ortiz, MD
Lisa Wishart Chaffin	*Cover Stylists*	Linda Smoak
	Sweet Pea Ellman	Ellen Nagel
Quilt Coordinator	Judy Mangasarian	Renee Belair
Joan T. Bounds		

Martha Anne Collins — *President 2007-08*

Liz Juerling — *President 2008-09*

SIMPLE STARTS

Appetizers and Cocktails

"The Villagers provided Fairchild Tropical Botanic Garden
with a grant to help restore the historic gatehouse."

THE VILLAGERS

SALMON PARTY BALL

Ingredients

1 pound canned salmon

8 ounce cream cheese, softened

1 tablespoon fresh lemon juice

2 teaspoons grated onion

1 teaspoon horseradish

¼ teaspoon salt

¼ teaspoon liquid smoke

3 tablespoons chopped parsley

½ cup chopped pecans

Cherry tomatoes and parsley sprigs for garnish

Crackers for serving

Directions

Combine salmon, cream cheese, lemon juice, onion, horseradish, salt and liquid smoke. Mix thoroughly and chill several hours.

Combine pecans and parsley. Shape salmon mixture into a ball or log, and roll in the nut mixture. Chill again. Serve with assorted crackers. Garnish with cherry tomatoes and parsley. Allow to stand at room temperature for easier spreading.

Serves 10 to 12

SCALLOP CEBICHE

Ingredients

2 pounds bay scallops

1 pickled or frozen Aji Mirasol chilie, or 2 fresh Serrano chilies

1 cup fresh key lime juice

1 teaspoon sea salt

1 small red bell pepper, seeded, finely chopped

6 scallions, white part only, finely chopped

¼ cup extra-virgin olive oil

3 tablespoons fresh cilantro, finely chopped

Directions

Place the scallops in a large bowl and rinse under cold running water to remove any sand. Strain in a large colander, coarsely chop, and return to the large bowl. Seed the Aji Mirasol or chilies, and cut into thin strips. Combine the chilies with the limejuice and sea salt in a small bowl. Add to the scallops and toss well to mix. Let the scallops marinate in this mixture in the refrigerator until they turn opaque and firmer to the touch, no more than 2-3 hours. Just before serving, mix in the bell pepper, scallions, olive oil, and cilantro.

Makes 4 to 6 servings

HUMMUS

with Tomatoes and Parsley

This is great to serve with warm pita bread or as a dip for vegetables.

Ingredients

1 14-ounce can chickpeas, drained, and rinsed well

2 tablespoons olive oil

2 tablespoons lemon juice

2 garlic cloves

2 tablespoons chopped parsley as a garnish

1 chopped, seeded tomato as a garnish

Directions

Blend the chickpeas, olive oil, lemon juice, and garlic cloves in a food processor or a blender until fairly smooth. Serve with the parsley and chopped tomatoes sprinkled on top.

Serves 6

HOMEMADE HUMMUS

Tahini is a sesame seed paste and gives the hummus a wonderful depth of flavor. You can also add some sun-dried tomato or roasted red pepper.

Ingredients

1 14-ounce can garbanzo beans, drained and rinsed

2-3 cloves garlic, chopped

½ cup sesame tahini

Squeeze of lemon juice

Couple of splashes of rice vinegar

Couple of splashes of olive oil

Sun dried tomatoes (optional)

Roasted red peppers (optional)

Directions

Mix all the ingredients together and gently pulse in a food processor or mix and mash by hand.

Serves 8

BUÑUELOS DE ESPINACA

This delicious recipe for spinach fritters is from Uruguay.

Ingredients

1 bag of fresh spinach or 1 package frozen spinach, thawed and drained

1 tomato, diced

1 onion, diced

2 tablespoons cooking oil

Salt (or garlic salt) and pepper to taste

2 tablespoons grated Parmesan cheese

1½ cups all-purpose flour

2 teaspoons baking powder

2 eggs, beaten

¾ cup milk

Oil for frying

Directions

Sauté the spinach, tomato, and onion in oil until tender. Add salt, pepper, and cheese. Mix well. Set aside to cool.

In a bowl, mix together the flour, ½ teaspoon salt, baking powder, eggs, and milk. Add spinach mixture and stir to combine thoroughly. Drop by spoonfuls into hot oil (360 degrees F) for 2 to 3 minutes until golden. Turn and fry for another minute.

Makes 36

SWEET ONION SPREAD

Ingredients

2 medium sweet onions, roughly chopped

2 teaspoons extra-virgin olive oil

2 teaspoons honey

4 large garlic cloves, peeled and smashed

Salt, to taste

Directions

Preheat oven to 350 degrees. Stir first 4 ingredients to coat. Put in greased baking dish. Bake uncovered for 1 hour. Stir occasionally, remove and let cool. Place in blender; add salt and blend until smooth.

Serve on toast points or crusty French bread. The spread can be refrigerated for up to one week.

Makes approximately 2 cups

CHINESE CHICKEN STICKS

This is a classic Chinese h'ors d'ouvres that is served with sweet and sour sauce.

Ingredients

20 chicken wing drumsticks

Garlic powder

½ cup flour

Oil for deep frying

2 tablespoons corn starch

½ teaspoon baking powder

½ cup cold water

¼ cup flour for dusting

Directions

Remove skin and any fat. Using kitchen shears cut the skin away from the base of the drumsticks and push the meat up into a ball at the top of the drumstick. Wash and pat dry chicken drumsticks. Season to taste with the garlic powder. Refrigerate until you're ready to fry. To make the batter, first sift together the ½ cup flour, cornstarch and the baking powder. Add the water just before you are ready to fry the drumsticks. Whisk to get a smooth batter. Dust the drumsticks with some flour. Dip the flour-dusted drumsticks into batter and deep fry at 350 degrees to a golden brown.

Serves 6

Sweet and Sour Sauce

⅔ cup pineapple juice

¼ cup rice vinegar, white or brown

½ cup sugar

½ cup catsup

1 teaspoon salt

2 tablespoons corn starch

1 tablespoon Worcestershire sauce

1 tablespoon white or black sesame seeds

Directions

Combine the first 5 ingredients in a small saucepan and mix well. Add cornstarch and whisk. When ready to serve bring these ingredients to a boil stirring constantly. Turn off heat and stir in Worcestershire sauce and sesame seeds. Serve as a dip to accompany the fried drumsticks.

CROSTINI PRIMAVERA

Although crostini can be bought at fine grocery stores, it will not be as fresh as homemade. The mozzarella adds the extra pizzazz.

Ingredients

1 loaf of skinny French bread

4 garlic cloves, peeled and finely diced

¼ cup extra virgin olive oil

2 to 3 red tomatoes (depending on size), seeds removed

1 yellow tomato, seeds removed

1 small bunch of fresh basil leaves

1 container fresh mozzarella cheese, small balls

Salt, to taste

Fresh ground pepper, to taste

Directions

Mix together the olive oil, garlic and a little salt. Let it sit for 30 minutes.

Remove mozzarella from liquid. Cut into thin slices and return to the refrigerator.

Cut bread on the diagonal into ¼ inch slices. Place on baking sheet that has been lined with aluminum foil. Brush garlic olive oil mixture on both sides of bread slices. Put under broiler for a couple of minutes or until golden. KEEP AN EYE ON THEM! They will burn very quickly. Remove, turn onto other side and repeat. Set aside to cool off.

Dice all the seeded tomatoes and put in a bowl. Add 2 teaspoons of the diced garlic that has been swimming in the olive oil. Stack 5 large basil leaves on top of each other, roll them up and cut into thin strips. Add the basil to the tomato/garlic mix. Drizzle a small amount of the garlic-infused olive oil over the mix. Add salt and pepper to taste. Refrigerate until a half hour before party time.

Assemble the crostini by placing a thin cheese slice on each crusty piece of bread. Spoon a small amount of tomato mixture on top. Arrange on a nice platter to serve.

Serves 8 to 10

GEORGIA CAVIAR

One of the favorites at Villager meetings.
Serve this very flavorful dip with the large scoop Fritos.

Ingredients

1 15-ounce can black eyed peas, rinsed

½ green pepper diced

½ red pepper diced

4 scallions chopped

1 8-ounce bottle zesty Italian dressing

Directions

Mix ingredients and cover with dressing. Marinate all-day or overnight.

Serves 4 to 6

GUACAMOLE DIP

Ingredients

3 ripe medium avocados

2 tablespoons olive oil

3 medium sweet tomatoes, finely chopped

2 tablespoons chopped onion, Vidalia or red onion

1 teaspoon sea salt

Pepper to taste

1 clove garlic, minced

Juice of 1 lemon

Directions

Peel and mash the avocados with a fork; add remaining ingredients. Place in an airtight container and chill until serving.

Serve with tortilla chips.

Serves 12

HAM AND CHEESE CRISPS

Shape and freeze these easy puff pastry appetizers days or weeks ahead, then bake just before serving. They're great!

Ingredients

1 7¼-ounce package frozen puff pastry (2 sheets)

2 tablespoons honey

2 tablespoons Dijon-style mustard

¼ cup grated Romano or Parmesan cheese

6 ounces thinly sliced fully cooked ham

1 egg

2 teaspoons water

Directions

Preheat oven to 400 degrees. Let folded pastry stand at room temperature for 20 minutes to thaw. Line the baking sheets with parchment or plain brown paper. Stir together the honey and mustard. Set aside.

On a lightly floured surface, unfold 1 pastry sheet. Spread with half of the honey-mustard mixture. Sprinkle with half of the cheese; top with half of the ham. Starting at a long edge, roll the pastry, jellyroll style, to center. Repeat from opposite edge, forming 2 rolls that meet in center. With a sharp knife, cut the pastry roll crosswise into ½ inch-thick slices. (If the roll is too soft to slice easily, chill for a few minutes.)

Arrange the slices 2 inches apart on the prepared baking sheets. Repeat with remaining pastry, honey-mustard mixture, cheese, and ham. Combine the egg and water; brush onto pastries. Bake pastries at 400 degrees for 15 to 18 minutes or until golden. Remove from sheet; cool on a rack. Serve warm or at room temperature.

Note: To freeze for later, place baking sheet with the pastries in the freezer until solid, transfer frozen pastries to freezer containers or bags. Freeze for up to 1 month.

Makes 40

HOT AND SPICY CHINESE SHRIMP

This is a simple party food that will go quickly!

Ingredients

2 pounds shelled raw shrimp

½ cup olive oil

2 or 3 cloves minced garlic

2 tablespoons crushed red pepper

3 green onions, chopped

¼ cup soy sauce

Directions

Heat the oil; add the garlic and red pepper. Add the green onions, and cook just about a minute. Add the shrimp and the soy sauce. Stir-fry until the shrimp is cooked through. Transfer to a serving dish and put toothpicks in the shrimp.

Tip: Don't forget a little bowl for used toothpicks!

Serves 6 to 8

YUMMY HORS D'OEUVRES

Ingredients

1 pound kielbasa

1 12-ounce bottle of beer

1 15-ounce can stewed tomatoes

1 jar Kikkoman sweet and sour dipping sauce

1 tablespoon lemon juice

Directions

Preheat oven to 350 degrees. Slice the kielbasa into ½ inch pieces. Pour the beer into a large skillet. Bring to a simmer and add kielbasa slices. Cook sausage for three minutes per side. Drain and place in a baking dish. Put the tomatoes, dipping sauce, and lemon juice in a blender. Blend and pour over the sliced kielbasa. Bake for 1 hour. Serve hot.

Serves 10

CHEESY OLIVE PUFFS

A Villager favorite. Serve them warm or at room temperature.

Ingredients

1 cup grated sharp cheddar cheese (about ¼ pound)

4 tablespoons butter, softened (½ stick)

½ cup all purpose flour

½ teaspoon salt, optional

½ teaspoon paprika

Dash of cayenne pepper

30 medium pimento-stuffed green olives, well drained

Directions

In food processor, combine the cheese, butter, flour, salt, paprika, and cayenne. Mix just until blended. The dough may be crumbly, but will come together due to the heat from your hands. Pinch off a small amount of the dough, flatten in your hand slightly, and wrap it around an olive. Roll the olive in your hands to smooth it out. Place each olive on a baking sheet.

When all the olives are wrapped, cover with plastic wrap and freeze for at least one hour.

Preheat oven to 375 degrees. When you're ready to bake the puffs, take pan with the puffs straight from the freezer, remove plastic wrap, and bake for 17 to 18 minutes, until browned.

Makes 30 puffs

DEVILED HAM

This mixture is great served on crackers or even as a filling for tea sandwiches.

Ingredients

3 cups cooked ham, cut into ¾ inch pieces

½ stick unsalted butter, softened

¼ cup Dijon mustard

¼ cup mango chutney

Directions

Pulse ham in food processor until finely chopped. Transfer to a bowl. Add butter, mustard and chutney to the processor and blend until smooth. Stir into ham.

Makes 4 cups

SPICY CAYENNE TOASTS

with Sun Dried Tomato Spread

These toasts are great for parties since the spread and the toasts can both be made ahead of time.

Ingredients

½ cup olive oil

2 teaspoons ground cayenne pepper

1 teaspoon salt

1 teaspoon sugar

½ teaspoon paprika

1½ teaspoons garlic powder

1 loaf French bread baguette, sliced into ¼ inch rounds

Directions

Preheat the oven to 200 degrees. In the container of a blender or food processor, or in a jar with a tight-fitting lid, combine the olive oil and seasonings, mixing well. Lay the bread slices on a cookie sheet. Brush one side lightly with the flavored oil. Bake 1 hour or until crisp. Cool. The toasts may be prepared ahead of time and frozen.

To serve, bring the mixture to room temperature and spread over the toasts.

Sun-Dried Tomato Spread

1½ ounces sun-dried tomatoes

¼ cup olive oil

2 cloves garlic, minced

1 tablespoon minced parsley

5 basil leaves, chopped

1 scallion, chopped

1 teaspoon freshly ground black pepper

½ teaspoon salt

Pinch of sugar

4 ounces goat cheese

Directions

To re-hydrate sun-dried tomatoes, place them in boiling water for 5 minutes. Drain. Mix the tomatoes with the remaining ingredients, except goat cheese, in a container and refrigerate for 4 hours. Process the refrigerated mixture with the goat cheese in a food processor until smooth.

Makes approximately 24 toasts

SPICED NUTS

This is a traditional favorite from the Stockhausen family cookbook.

Ingredients

½ cup sugar

¼ teaspoon cloves

¼ teaspoon allspice

¼ teaspoon cinnamon

1 egg white, stiffly beaten

1½ teaspoons water

2 cups pecan halves

Directions

Preheat oven to 250 degrees. Add first four ingredients to the stiffly beaten egg whites. Add the water. Mix in the pecan halves. Spread on a cookie sheet and bake for one hour. With a spatula, turn over every 15 minutes while baking.

Store in an airtight container.

Makes 2 cups

SPICY ALMONDS

The basic seasonings can be used with walnuts, pecans, cooked chickpeas or pumpkin seeds. Store the nuts in an airtight box or tin.

Ingredients

3 tablespoons peanut oil

2 cups blanched almonds

½ cup plus 1 tablespoon granulated sugar

1½ teaspoons salt

1½ tablespoons ground cumin

1 teaspoon hot pepper flakes

Directions

Heat oil in heavy bottom frying pan over medium-high heat. Add the almonds, and sprinkle the ½ cup granulated sugar over them. Sauté until the almonds are golden brown and the sugar caramelizes.

Remove almonds and toss in a bowl with the salt, cumin, pepper flakes and remaining 1 tablespoon sugar.

Makes 2 cups

"WHY I FELL IN LOVE" BRIE

Ingredients

1 package of Pillsbury croissant rolls

1 4-inch or 5-inch diameter Brie

1 6-ounce jar of guava shells

Directions

Preheat oven to 400 degrees. Spray a cookie sheet with Pam spray or equivalent. Open croissant dough and unroll, placing on a flat, floured surface. Flatten with your fingers, and place Brie in center of the dough. Open the jar of guava shells, and drain into a bowl, saving the syrup in the jar. Arrange guava shells on top of the Brie so that the top is covered. Fold the croissant dough up and around the Brie and guava shells until they are completely enclosed. Pinch any open areas closed. Place on a greased pan. Brush top with a little of the saved guava syrup.

Bake the Brie in the oven for 15 to 20 minutes, or until the crust is brown. Let cool for ten minutes, then slice into pie sized wedges. Serve with French bread slices or crackers.

Serves 8 adults or 4 sweet-toothers!

Fairchild Tropical Gardens

SPICED CHILLED WINE

Although the orange blossom water will give a wonderful flavor, you can substitute it for one juiced orange and one sliced orange.

Ingredients

1 24-ounce bottle
dry white or red wine

2 peeled quarter size
slices fresh ginger

5 whole cloves

1 tablespoon sugar

2 tablespoons orange
blossom water

1 juiced lemon, 1 sliced lemon

½ teaspoon freshly
ground nutmeg

1 cinnamon stick

1 small ripe peach, nectarine,
apple, cut in wedges

Directions

Combine in a glass jar or pitcher. Let sit overnight, or longer, in the refrigerator.

When serving, put a few ice cubes in each individual glass. Fill each glass ¾ full of spiced wine, and top with seltzer and lemon soda to taste. Stir the contents of each glass and serve. Place the unused spiced wine back in the refrigerator.

Yields about 10 servings

CARMELLA'S KAHLUA

Ingredients

3 cups of sugar

1 cup powdered coffee

2 ounces vanilla

1½ cups water

1/5 of vodka

Directions

Mix first 4 ingredients together in a pan and boil over medium heat. Cool completely and pour into a half-gallon container. Add the fifth of vodka.

Makes 10 cups

MANGO MARGARITAS

Ingredients

1 26-ounce jar sliced mangoes, un-drained

A few tablespoons colored decorator sugar

1 6-ounce can frozen limeade concentrate, thawed

1 cup Gold Tequila

½ cup Triple Sec or Cointreau

¼ cup Grand Marnier

crushed ice

Directions

Spoon 3 tablespoons of the mango liquid from the jar into a shallow saucer. To prepare the drinking glasses, place the sugar in another shallow saucer and dip the rims of glasses into the mango liquid and then into the sugar.

Pour mangoes and remaining liquid into an electric blender. Add limeade and next 3 ingredients to blender. Process until smooth. Pour half of the mixture into a small pitcher and set aside for use in the second batch.

Add crushed ice to the mixture remaining in blender, bringing it to a 5 cup level. Process again until smooth.

Pour the blender mixture into glasses and serve.

Repeat with the remaining mango mixture in the pitcher and more ice.

Yields 10 cups

BLUEBERRY VODKA

Ingredients

Good Quality Vodka

Organic Blueberry Juice

Ginger ale

Directions

Mix ⅓ of each into a pitcher. Or, mix according to taste. You may want to use more ginger ale and less blueberry juice.

ANIMAL CRACKERS IN MY SOUP

Soups and Chowders

"In 2008, the Village of Pinecrest restored the 1936 entrance to the original Parrot Jungle with assistance from a Villager grant."

THE VILLAGERS

QUEEN MABEL'S CHOWDER

In the Bahamas, fish and conch chowders are served throughout the islands. *In the late 1950s, during a sailboat trip across the Gulf Stream to the Bahamas from Key Biscayne, we stopped for some days at Frazier's Hog Cay where matriarch Queen Mabel greeted us, proclaiming, "I am Queen Mabel and I rules the Island." She taught me how to make basic chowders. Of course she did not measure – and that's my favorite kind of recipe.*

Grouper is the fish of choice for Queen Mabel. She used the head (including the eyes) but it can be made with the de-boned fillet. Queen Mabel began with a good-sized kettle (preferably iron) or cooking pot, rubbing its bottom with a piece of salt pork. She filled the pot about two-thirds full of water, added a splash of fresh sea water and then put it over a driftwood fire on the beach. She said "put in plenty onions and potatoes and a handful of hot chilies" (Queen Mabel picked her tiny red peppers from what we called her burning bush). She said if she had celery or carrots she'd add them, and she laughed, "Somedays them black-eyed peas floats round my chowder." Generous with her grouper, she said it was firm so best for chowders. She never added tomato.

Over the ensuing years, I have made many variations of this chowder, and added different ingredients (see below) and sometimes drop in shrimp and scallops just before serving. It also works for conch chowder. It has little resemblance to tomato or cream chowders. And chowders are always best the second day.

The core of any fish soup or chowder is its fish stock. It's worth the time to make your own. Depending on your bravery quotient, you can ask your fishmonger to give you a grouper head complete with eyeballs, which makes a richer stock for chowders (just wrap the head in cheesecloth to keep the bones separate). Make it at your convenience and freeze it so you will always have some on hand.

Fish Stock

4 to 5 cups water, lightly salted

½ pound shrimp shells

½ pound fresh white fish, chopped

¼ onion, chopped

1 carrot, chopped

1 celery stalk, chopped

8 sprigs parsley

½ lime, juiced

1 teaspoon ground black pepper

Directions

Combine all and simmer for 30 or more minutes, stir, cool and strain. Cover and refrigerate. Freeze it if you are not going to use the next day.

2½ medium onions, chopped into large bite size pieces

4 cups water

Sea salt, fresh ground pepper to taste

8 sprigs parsley

1 jalapeno, whole

4½ medium potatoes, chopped into large bite size pieces

4 cups warm fish stock (see previous page)

½ eggplant, coarsely chopped

1 whole carrot

2 celery stalks

2 inch piece of fresh ginger, peeled

1 whole corn on the cob, shucked

1 tablespoon butter

4 Key limes

1½ pounds grouper fillets, carefully boned

½ medium potato, cut into big chunks

½ medium onion, cut into big chunks

2 shots of dark rum, optional

1 bunch cilantro, chopped for garnish

1 medium onion, finely chopped for garnish

Chili peppers, for garnish

Sliced Key limes

Directions

Season a cast iron cooking pot with olive oil or a piece of salt pork rubbed on its bottom to melt, and ground pepper. Sizzle 1 of the chopped onions until translucent. Add 4 cups of water, salt, half of the parsley sprigs, jalapeno, and bring to a boil. Add potatoes and the rest of the onions, reduce to a medium simmer.

After 20 minutes add 4 cups warm fish stock, return to a simmer for about 30 minutes. Add eggplant, whole carrot, celery stalk, the rest of the parsley sprigs, and ginger. Return to a low boil and add corn on the cob, a dash of salt and the butter. After 5 minutes readjust to a low simmer for 30 minutes. Squeeze juice from Key limes on grouper fillets and rub fish with black pepper. Return ½ pound of the grouper to the refrigerator. Turn up the heat, and add the pound of prepared grouper to the pot. As the fish begins to cook, stir, and adjust temperature back to a low-simmer for 2 or 3 hours. Turn off heat and let chowder stand. When it is cooler, remove jalapeno, parsley sprigs, ginger, celery stalks, and carrot. Remove corn on the cob.

Put 2 cups of the chowder in a food processor, blend until smooth, return to chowder and raise heat to simmer. Put ½ medium potato and onion into the food processor and grind; stir the pulp into chowder. Cover and simmer for 10 minutes to thicken and heighten the flavor. When hot, add final grouper to chowder: cover and simmer for 10 minutes. Stir and taste to adjust seasoning. Add the double shot of dark rum, if desired, and a good squeeze of lime. Serve with garnishes on side.

Serves 4

JOAN GILL BLANK'S FABULOUS FISH SOUP

Coastal and island fishing villages around the world are famous for dishes using local fish and shellfish. Traditionally in Florida, grouper, shrimp and squid are among the mainstays of regional seafood soups and chowders. There are three steps to creating this tomato-based zupa: sauce, stock, & seafood. Prepare the tomato-based sauce the day before.

Tomato Sauce for Fish Soup

1 tablespoon olive oil

1 tablespoon butter

1 medium onion

3 minced garlic cloves

1 stalk celery

½ stalk fresh fennel

2 to 3 jalapenos

6 large leaves whole fresh basil

8 sprigs parsley

1 stem fresh oregano

1 red chili pepper

1 whole clove

Fresh ground black pepper to taste

4 ounces dry white wine

3 dashes Tabasco

3 dashes Worcestershire

2 tablespoons good red wine vinegar

4 8-ounce cans tomato sauce

1 bay leaf

½ teaspoon ground black pepper

Directions

Chop all the dry ingredients into small pieces and sauté in olive oil and butter until you begin to smell the aroma. Do not overcook.

Add the wine, Tabasco, Worcestershire, vinegar, tomato sauce, bay leaf, and ground black pepper.

Keep at a low simmer for 2 hours, stirring occasionally. Turn off the heat and smell the aromas. Cover and refrigerate.

Tomato Sauce for Fish Soup
(previous page)

2½ cups Fish Stock (page 34)

¼ cup dry white wine

½ pound fresh grouper fillets
cut into 1 to 2 inch cubes

8 large shrimp, or
4 langoustines if available,
shelled (you can use the
shells for the stock)

8 mussels

1¼-pints scallops,
cut into ½ or ¼ inch pieces

1 king crab leg,
divided into 2 inch pieces

2 or 3 squid, sliced into ¼ inch
rounds, plus tentacles divided
in half

Florida crawfish,
if in season, optional

4 sprigs parsley, for garnish

4 Key limes, sliced, for garnish

4 slices of thick country-style
rosemary bread drizzled with
olive oil, toasted

Directions

Simmer the tomato sauce in a pot; add 2 ½ cups of the hot fish stock 10 minutes before serving. Add the white wine and stir. Add the grouper, shrimp, mussels, scallops, crab legs.

Simmer a couple of minutes until the mussel shells open, then take the pan off the fire.

Add the squid, which will cook in the residual heat. Ladle soup into bowls.

Top with a crab leg, a sprig of parsley, and a slice of Key Lime. Serve the bread on the side.

Serves 4

3 BEAN SOUP

Ingredients

**2 chicken breasts,
skinned but still on the bone**

3 cups water

1 28-ounce can whole tomatoes

**1 10-ounce package frozen
green beans**

**1 10-ounce package frozen
baby lima beans**

**1 15-ounce can black or
great northern beans**

1 bay leaf

2 teaspoons Creole seasoning

1 teaspoon chili powder

**4 teaspoons each of
garlic powder, onion powder,
and red pepper**

**Dash of hot sauce, soy sauce
and Worcestershire sauce**

Directions

Cook the chicken in the water at a boil, take it out and cut it up. Remove the bones. Place de-boned chicken and the rest of the ingredients back into the pot. Simmer on low for an hour or two.

Yields about 12 cups

The Original Parrot Jungle Entrance

AVOCADO SOUP

with Shrimp

Ingredients

3 large avocados, peeled and cut into chunks

28 ounces of Imagine No-Chicken broth or Swanson's vegetable broth

¼ teaspoon ground red pepper

1 teaspoon salt

½ cup buttermilk

3 tablespoons lemon juice

¼ cup dry white wine

½ pound medium peeled, cooked shrimp

1 tablespoon olive oil

1 teaspoon lemon zest

1 tablespoon lemon juice

¾ teaspoon salt

Chopped fresh chives for garnish

Directions

Process the first four ingredients in a blender. Transfer to a bowl and stir in the buttermilk, lemon juice, and wine. Place plastic wrap directly on the soup and chill for one to four hours.

Slice shrimp in half, lengthwise. Combine shrimp, olive oil, lemon zest, lemon juice and salt. Let stand for 15 minutes.

Ladle the soup into bowls, garnish with shrimp and chives.

Serves 6

CHARLIE FROW'S CHOWDER

John Frow owned the property just south of Charlie Peacock's property in Coconut Grove. In 1887, he sold it to Ralph Munroe, Commodore of the Biscayne Bay Yacht Club, which had been founded that same year. John Frow had been a keeper of the Cape Florida lighthouse. His son Charlie Frow was the Biscayne Bay Yacht Club's lamplighter, for which he received payment of $1.50 a month in about 1891. By the early 1900s, Charlie had become the club's chowder maker, a culinary art he had learned from Charles Peacock.

Ingredients

1 pound salt pork, skin off, ¼ inch cubes

1 pound onions, chopped

¼ green pepper, chopped

1 quart chicken or turkey stock

1 can tomato soup

4 large potatoes, peeled, cut into ½ inch cubes

4 pounds fish, no skin, no bones, cut into cubes

2 tablespoons butter

2 tall cans evaporated milk

Tabasco to taste

1 bay leaf

¼ teaspoon thyme

Salt and white pepper to taste

Directions

Brown the salt pork, add onions and green pepper, and sauté briefly. Add the stock, tomato soup and potatoes. Cook slowly about 10 minutes. Add the fish and cook slowly until fish is flaky, about another 10 minutes. Add butter, milk, seasonings, and simmer briefly. Season to taste.

Serves 12

BUTTERNUT SQUASH PARSNIP SOUP

Ingredients

1 3 to 4-pound butternut squash

1 Granny Smith apple, peeled, cored, and quartered

2 tablespoons butter

2 tablespoons olive oil

1 large sweet onion, chopped

3 parsnips, peeled and chopped

1½ teaspoons salt

1 teaspoon pepper

5 cups low-sodium fat-free chicken broth

¼ cup whipping cream

⅛ teaspoon paprika

⅛ teaspoon ground cumin

Sour cream for garnish

Directions

Preheat oven to 400 degrees. Cut squash in half and remove seeds. Place squash, cut sides down, and quartered apples on a lightly greased aluminum foil-lined baking sheet.

Bake for 45 minutes or until squash pulp is tender. Remove from oven; cool. Scoop out squash pulp, discarding shells.

Melt butter in olive oil in a large Dutch oven over medium heat; add onion, parsnips, salt and pepper, and sauté 20 minutes, or until onion is caramel colored. Add squash, apple quarters, and chicken broth, and bring to a boil. Reduce heat to medium, and simmer, stirring often, 10 minutes. Remove from heat; cool.

Process squash mixture, in batches, in a blender or food processor until smooth, stopping to scrape down sides. Return to Dutch oven. Stir in whipping cream, paprika, and cumin, and simmer 5 to 10 minutes or until heated. Garnish, if desired, with sour cream and paprika.

Serves 6 to 8

COLD CUCUMBER SOUP

A soup that is ideal for those hot summer days in August (up north, when the cucumbers are ripe) or anytime in Florida. This soup gets better with age and is really at its best on the 2nd or 3rd day! This is a favorite on the buffet table and is always a hit at the Villager garden tours.

Ingredients

3 cucumbers, peeled, cut in half-length wise, seeded then cut into chunks

4 celery stalks diced

2 carrots, peeled and sliced into chunks

1 large onion, diced (Vidalia or sweet)

3 cloves garlic, sliced

1 quart container of organic chicken stock

2 to 4 tablespoons of dried dill weed

2 containers of sour cream

Directions

In a pressure cooker add all the vegetables, garlic, ½ of the chicken stock and one heaping handful of dill weed. Cook on high for 5 minutes.
(If not using pressure cooker, cover veggies with stock and simmer covered until all veggies are soft about 25 minutes.)

Pour the cooked soup and an equal amount of sour cream into a blender or food processor and puree. Add some of the extra stock for thinning. When all ingredients are well blended, pour into a large container, add remaining dill and stir well.

Place soup in refrigerator for 24 hours. Serve cold, in a bowl, garnish with dill.

Serves 10 to 12

COLD SHRIMP SOUP

Ingredients

1 pound small cooked shrimp,
cut into small pieces

1 large cucumber, peeled,
seeded and diced

1 cup fresh tomatoes, peeled,
seeded and diced

1 quart buttermilk

Salt, white pepper,
and Tabasco to taste

2 tablespoons chopped dill

2 tablespoons chopped chives

Directions

Mix together and chill overnight, covered,
in a non-metal container.

Serves 10 to 12

CRAB AND SWEET POTATO SOUP

*This is the signature soup of "Fiddleheads Restaurant" in
Glens Falls, NY. This soup is worth it!*

Ingredients

¼ cup unsalted butter

¼ cup each of carrot, celery,
and onion, diced

½ cup flour

1 tablespoon Old Bay Seasoning

1½ quarts hot chicken stock

4 cups sweet potatoes, peeled,
medium diced

1 cup heavy cream

1 pound Maryland
lump crab meat

Directions

On medium high heat in a large pot, sauté the
vegetables in butter. Add the flour and Old Bay,
and stir for 1 minute.

Add hot stock and whisk until smooth, reduce heat
and add potatoes. Cook until tender. Stir in the
cream and crabmeat. Simmer for five minutes.

Makes 16 cups

GAZPACHO

Ingredients

1½ tablespoons wine vinegar

¼ cup olive oil

2 cloves garlic

1 cucumber, peeled, seeded, cut into small cubes

1 green pepper, seeded, cut into small pieces

3 scallions, chopped

½ teaspoon Worcestershire

½ cup water

2 teaspoons salt

¼ teaspoon pepper

8 ripe tomatoes

Toasted croutons

Directions

Put all ingredients except the tomatoes and croutons into a blender. Pulse several times, until all ingredients are coarsely chopped. Empty into a large bowl.

Place tomatoes in a pot of boiling water and simmer 5 minutes, depending on how ripe the tomatoes are. Remove and immediately put tomatoes into a bowl of cold water. Remove the tomato skins, cut in half, core, and seed. Cut skinned tomatoes into large pieces and blend until coarsely chopped. Add to the other vegetables in the bowl. Serve chilled with croutons and additional cucumber garnish if desired.

Serves 6

PASTA FAGIOLI

Ingredients

1 pound Great Northern beans

4 quarts water

½ cup olive oil

3 tablespoons minced garlic

2 tablespoons tomato paste

2 tablespoons salt

½ teaspoon dried basil

½ teaspoon dried oregano

½ pound small shell macaroni, cooked

Freshly ground pepper

Freshly grated Parmesan cheese

Directions

Boil beans with the water over high heat for 15 minutes. Add olive oil, minced garlic, tomato paste, salt, basil and oregano. Continue cooking until beans are tender, about 1¼ hours. Add more water if necessary. Stir in cooked macaroni. Add Parmesan cheese and pepper. Serve hot.

Serves 8-10

KAY'S GYPSY SOUP

Ingredients

1 pound lean ground beef

1 28-ounce jar chunky spaghetti sauce with mushrooms and green peppers

1 cup chopped onion

1 cup sliced celery

1 clove garlic, crushed, or 1 teaspoon garlic powder

½ to 1 tablespoon sugar

½ tablespoon salt

¼ teaspoon Creole seasoning

1 14½-ounce can beef broth

2 cups water

1 cup tomato juice or chicken broth

1 10-ounce can diced tomatoes with chilies

1 12-ounce package frozen mixed vegetables

Directions

In a Dutch oven over medium-high heat, cook the ground beef until it is brown, breaking it up with a wooden spoon as it cooks. Put in a colander, discard the fat and rinse in the sink with hot water. Put back in the pot and add the chunky spaghetti sauce, onion, celery, garlic, sugar, salt, Creole seasoning, beef broth and water.

Bring to a boil over high heat, reduce heat, and simmer 10 minutes. Add the tomato juice or chicken broth. Add the diced tomatoes and frozen vegetables. Return to a boil, and reduce heat and simmer 20 minutes.

Makes about 12 cups

MUSHROOM SOUP

A melt-in-your-mouth soup that is well worth the effort.

Ingredients

2 to 3 tablespoons butter (use only European unsweetened!)

1 pint of Crimini or baby Portobello mushrooms, sliced evenly

1 tablespoon extra virgin olive oil

1 pint heavy whipping cream

Directions

Heat the butter in a pot over medium heat. When the butter just starts to turn brown on the edges, add the sliced mushrooms and the olive oil. Sauté on medium heat, and cook until they are tender. Add salt and pepper to taste, as the mushrooms finish cooking. Never add the salt to the mushrooms too early. Wait until they are done or you will make them soggy with the salt.

Put the cooked mushrooms in a blender, drizzle in the cream as you blend until a light frothy consistency is achieved. Remove the small inner lid from the top of the blender and cover it with a kitchen towel as you blend the mushrooms and cream, to let heat out. The heat of the mushrooms should heat the cream to the perfect temperature.

Serve immediately.

Makes 4 cups

HATTIE'S SOUTHERN GUMBO

Hattie was Joan La Roche's "kissin' cousin" from Alabama.
She lived on the Mobile River, would trap the crabs herself,
and grew everything else in her garden. This is the real thing!

Ingredients

1 cup cooking oil

1 cup all-purpose flour

8 stalks celery, chopped

3 large onions, chopped

1 green pepper, chopped

2 cloves garlic, minced

½ cup parsley, chopped

1 pound okra, sliced,
fresh or frozen

2 tablespoons shortening

2 quarts chicken stock

2 quarts water

½ cup Worcestershire sauce

Tabasco to taste

½ cup ketchup

1 large ripe tomato, chopped

2 teaspoons salt

4 slices cooked bacon or
1 large ham slice, chopped

2 bay leaves

¼ teaspoon thyme

¼ teaspoon rosemary

Red pepper flakes to taste

2 cups cooked chicken chopped,
optional

2 to 4 pounds cook shrimp

1 or 2 pounds cooked crabmeat

1 pint oysters (may used canned)

1 teaspoon molasses
or brown sugar

Lemon juice, if desired

Enough cooked rice for 12

Directions

Heat oil in a heavy iron pot over medium heat.
Add the flour very slowly, stirring constantly with
a wooden spoon until flour is medium brown. This
will take approximately 30 to 40 minutes.

Add the celery, onions, green pepper, garlic and
parsley. Reduce heat to low and cook an additional
45 minutes to 1 hour, stirring constantly. In a
saucepan, fry the okra in the shortening until
brown. Add to gumbo and stir well.

Add the chicken stock, water, Worcestershire
sauce, Tabasco, ketchup, chopped tomatoes, salt,
bacon or ham, bay leaves, thyme, rosemary and red
pepper flakes. Simmer on low for 2½ to 3 hours.

About 30 minutes before serving, add cooked
chicken (if desired), and shrimp and continue
simmering. Add crabmeat and oysters along
with molasses or brown sugar during the last 10
minutes of simmering. A bit of lemon juice may be
added at the very end if desired.

Put a generous amount of hot cooked rice in soup
bowls, spoon gumbo over rice and serve.

Yields 12 large servings

LENTIL SOUP

"It's Raining Outside and I Have the Sniffles"

Instead of dumplings, the soup may also be served over a bed of jasmine rice as a main course. The soup is high in protein and delicious.

Ingredients

1 medium onion, chopped

2 tablespoons olive oil

8½ cups water

1 pound package of dried lentils

5 celery stalks, chopped

3 ham hocks

3 carrots, chopped

Salt pepper to taste

¼ teaspoon cumin, to taste

¼ teaspoon parsley, to taste

¼ teaspoon whole oregano, to taste

Directions

In a large crock-pot, sauté the onions in olive oil until they are transparent, then add 8½ cups of water. Add the lentils, celery, ham hocks, carrots, salt and pepper, cumin, parsley, oregano and season to taste. Bring to a boil, stirring constantly, then lower the temperature to a simmer. Simmer, covered for two hours, stirring every fifteen minutes.

When almost ready to serve, briefly bring soup back to a boil to make the dumplings.

Serves 10

Dumplings

⅔ cup flour

1 egg

⅛ teaspoon salt

Directions

Mix the flour, egg and salt together. Drop by spoonfuls into the boiling soup. This will make dumplings that will float to the surface.

THAI-STYLE PUMPKIN SOUP

Ingredients

2 16-ounce cans fat-free, chicken broth

1 15-ounce can pureed pumpkin

1 12-ounce can mango nectar

2 tablespoons rice vinegar

1½ tablespoons minced green onion

1 teaspoon grated peeled fresh ginger

½ teaspoon grated orange rind

¼ teaspoon crushed red pepper

1 garlic clove, crushed

Chopped fresh cilantro

Directions

Combine first 3 ingredients in a large Dutch oven, and bring to a boil. Cover, reduce heat and simmer 10 minutes. Stir in the vinegar and next 5 ingredients; cook 3 minutes or until thoroughly heated. Ladle into soup bowls. Sprinkle with cilantro.

Makes 6 servings

POTAGE OF TURNIPS, LEEKS AND POTATOES

Ingredients

1½ tablespoons butter

6 cups ½-inch cubed Yukon gold or red potatoes (about 2 pounds)

3 cups ½-inch cubed peeled turnips (about 1 ¼ pounds)

2 cups chopped leek (about 2 large)

4½ cups water, divided

1½ teaspoons salt

5 thyme sprigs

2 tablespoons chopped fresh parsley

2 teaspoons chopped fresh thyme

½ teaspoon black pepper

10 cups coarsely chopped turnip greens (about ½ pounds)

½ cup (2-ounces) grated Gruyere cheese

Directions

Melt butter in a Dutch oven over medium heat. Add the potatoes, turnips, leek, and ½ cup water. Cover and cook 10 minutes, stirring occasionally. Add the other 4 cups of water, salt, and thyme sprigs; bring to a boil. Reduce heat; simmer, uncovered 25 minutes or until vegetables are very tender. Discard the thyme sprigs. Stir in the parsley, chopped thyme, and pepper.
(At this point, I used my submersion blender and pureed the entire mess.)

Cook turnip greens in boiling water in a large saucepan 5 minutes or until tender; drain well. Stir them into the potato mixture. Ladle soup into serving bowl; sprinkle with the grated cheese.

Serves 7

BLACK BEAN SOUP

There's nothing like a hearty soup to satisfy a group.
Serve with cornbread and a salad.

Ingredients

¼ pound bacon, diced

⅛ cup olive oil

2 fresh jalapeno peppers, seeded and diced

1 onion, diced

1 carrot, diced

3 celery stalks, diced

½ to 1 green pepper, diced

4 garlic cloves, minced

1 teaspoon cumin

2 smoked ham hocks

2 bay leafs

1 teaspoon oregano

4 15-ounce cans beans

½ cup Madeira or dry sherry

8 cups vegetable stock

Salt and pepper to taste

½ teaspoon Tabasco

1 teaspoon wine vinegar

Directions

Heat olive oil in a large stockpot over medium-low heat. Add the bacon and sauté, stirring occasionally, until browned, about 15 minutes. Add the jalapeno, onion, carrot, and garlic to the pot and sauté, uncovered, stirring occasionally, until the vegetables are soft but not browned, about 10 minutes.

Add the beans to the pot along with the 8 cups of stock (use the liquid from the beans to make up the 8 cups) and the bay leaves. Reduce the heat to medium low and simmer, uncovered, until the beans are tender and the vegetables have practically dissolved, 1 to 1½-hours. Stir the soup occasionally to make sure the beans aren't sticking to the pot.

Turn off the heat and season with salt, pepper, Tabasco, dry sherry, and vinegar.

Remove the bay leaves.

Serves 8

Garnish

3 tablespoons flat leaf parsley, or 1½ tablespoons cilantro, chopped

1 jalapeno, seeded, finely diced

½ cup sour cream

¼ red onion, finely diced

Toasted pumpkin seeds

Lime wedges

Directions

Mix together the garnish (can be made ahead and refrigerated) and serve with the soup.

EAT YOUR GREENS

Salads and Such

"In 1977, the Villagers helped restore El Jardin's courtyard patio (now a part of Carrollton School) to its original 1918 appearance."

THE VILLAGERS

SWEDISH WEST COAST SEAFOOD SALAD

No, we're not talking California. This is a famous salad from the west coast of Sweden. It is often served at elegant post-theatre suppers. If you wish, you can add lobster to the salad for even more delicious flavor. It's great to serve at a Ladies' Luncheon, or on a buffet table.

Ingredients

8 ounces cooked, peeled, shrimp

10 to 15 (blue) mussels or 1 can of mussels

1 bunch fresh asparagus or 1 can white asparagus

3 tomatoes

2 hard-boiled eggs cut into wedges

8 ounces fresh mushrooms

½ large cucumber

1 lemon, sliced, for garnish

¾ cup frozen green peas, thawed

1 small head iceberg lettuce

Directions

Begin by cooking the shrimp and mussels if they are raw. Blanch the asparagus if fresh, and chill. Cut the tomatoes and eggs into wedges. Set aside the eggs for garnish. Slice the mushrooms, cucumber, and lemon. Peel the shrimp. Cut the asparagus in thirds.

Mix the asparagus, tomatoes, mushrooms, cucumbers and peas with the shrimp and toss with some Rhode Island Sauce. Tear the iceberg lettuce into good-sized pieces and cover sides and bottom of a large salad bowl.

Mound the dressed vegetables and shrimp in the salad bowl. Finally, garnish with the mussels and eggs. Drizzle some more sauce over the mussels and eggs. Garnish with the lemon slices.

Pair with Rhode Island Sauce (found on page 55), or your favorite vinaigrette.

Serves 4-6

RHODE ISLAND SAUCE

Instead of the chili sauce you can cut up a bunch of fresh dill, squeeze a quarter of a juicy lemon, and mix with the mayonnaise and sour cream.

Ingredients

½ cup mayonnaise

½ cup sour cream

2 tablespoons chili sauce

Directions

Blend all the ingredients together in a dish. Season, if desired, with salt and pepper.

Serve with Swedish West Coast Salad or any Seafood Salad.

TONI'S VINAIGRETTE

This is a versatile dressing. Use it as a marinade for grilled vegetables, or alongside grilled fish or meats.

Ingredients

1 unpeeled clove of garlic

1 heaping teaspoon Villager Mango Chutney

3 tablespoons balsamic vinegar

3 tablespoons extra virgin olive oil

Directions

Place unpeeled clove of garlic in microwave on high for 7 seconds. Peel and finely chop. Combine chopped garlic with Villager mango chutney, balsamic vinegar, and extra virgin olive oil.

Yields approximately ⅓ cup

ALMOND CRUSTED CHICKEN SALAD

Ingredients

1 pound chicken breast, cut in long strips

Freshly ground black pepper

1 egg

1 tablespoon Kikkoman Teriyaki Marinade and Sauce

½ cup all purpose flour

½ cup Panko breadcrumbs

½ cup smoked almonds, finely chopped

2 to 3 tablespoons vegetable oil

6 cups mixed baby salad greens

2 oranges, peeled and cut into segments

Directions

Season the chicken with pepper. Beat the egg with teriyaki sauce in shallow bowl until well blended. Place the flour in a shallow dish. Combine breadcrumbs and almonds, and place in another shallow dish.

Dust both sides of the chicken with flour, then dip into the egg mixture and finally coat with the almond/breadcrumbs mixture. In a 12-inch skillet, heat 2 tablespoons vegetable oil over medium high heat. Add chicken and cook 6 to 7 minutes or until no longer pink in the center, turning over once and adding more oil as needed.

Divide salad greens among 4 dinner plates. Arrange chicken and orange segments onto the greens. Serve with the Orange Teriyaki Honey dressing.

Serves 4

Orange Teriyaki Honey Dressing

¼ cup Kikkoman Teriyaki Marinade and Sauce

¼ cup olive oil

2 tablespoons honey

2 tablespoons vinegar

1 teaspoon freshly grated orange peel

Directions

Whisk all the ingredients together to make the dressing. Refrigerate.

ENDIVE SALAD

with Pear and Walnuts

Ingredients

2 to 3 heads of endive sliced lengthwise in thin slices

2 cups arugula leaves

1 large perfectly ripe pear, chopped into small pieces

1 cup sugared walnut halves

1 cup crumbled maytag blue cheese or other fine blue cheese

Directions

Toss the arugula, endive, and vinaigrette together in a large salad bowl.

To serve, arrange the greens on 4 salad plates; top with the pear slices, walnuts and cheese.

Serves 4

Raspberry Vinaigrette

1 tablespoon dijon mustard

2 tablespoons raspberry vinegar or champagne vinegar

1 tablespoon orange or lemon juice

3 tablespoons extra virgin olive oil

Salt and freshly ground pepper to taste

Directions

In a large measuring cup, whisk all of the vinaigrette ingredients briskly until emulsified.

BLACK BEAN SALAD

Villager meetings always include food, and this is one of the favorites!
No one should be expected to work on an empty stomach.

Ingredients

2 15-ounce cans black beans, rinsed and drained

1 16-ounce can whole kernel corn, drained

1 each small green, yellow, and red sweet pepper, cut into 1 inch long strips

2 medium tomatoes, seeded, and cut into ½ inch pieces

2 stalks celery, sliced, about 1 cup

4 green onions, sliced, about ½ cup

¾ cup Italian salad dressing

¾ cup medium salsa

8 ounce orzo pasta, cooked and drained

Directions

Combine all the ingredients together in a large bowl. Cover and chill for 4 to 48 hours, stirring occasionally.

Serves 12

BROCCOLI SALAD

To make this a vegetarian salad, omit the bacon and add sunflower seeds.
This salad is always the first thing to go on our buffet table.

Ingredients

½ - ⅔ cup raisins

1 - 2 bunches of fresh broccoli, chopped, using part of the stem

1 medium red onion, chopped

½ to 1 pound bacon, cooked crisp and chopped (microwave bacon is perfect for this, it doesn't grease up your whole house)

½ cup sunflower seeds (optional)

Directions

Plump the raisins in a bowl with boiling water for a few minutes and drain well. Mix broccoli, raisins, bacon and onion together, add dressing and refrigerate.

Let sit for several hours or best overnight, covered in the refrigerator.

Serves 6

Dressing

1 cup mayonnaise

¼ cup sugar

2 tablespoons cider vinegar

Directions

To make the dressing, combine the mayonnaise, sugar and vinegar. Add to the salad and mix well to coat.

AMY'S SALAD

Ingredients

2 bags of baby spinach

½ cup roasted pumpkin seeds

½ cup crumbled feta or goat cheese

¼ cup extra virgin olive oil, to taste

3 tablespoons red wine vinegar, to taste

Directions

Combine the spinach with the pumpkin seeds and cheese. Drizzle the olive oil over salad. Add a few splashes of red wine vinegar, and toss the salad. Salt and pepper to taste.

Serves 4

WISHART FAMILY HERBED TOMATOES

Ingredients

8 ripe plum tomatoes

1¼ teaspoons salt

¼ teaspoon pepper

¾ teaspoon dried leaf thyme

⅓ cup minced fresh parsley

⅓ cup minced chives

¾ cup salad oil

⅓ cup tarragon vinegar

Directions

Blanch the tomatoes in boiling water for 30 seconds. Rinse under cold water. Peel the tomatoes and place in a bowl. Sprinkle with seasonings and herbs. Combine the oil and vinegar and pour over the tomatoes. Cover and chill for 2 hours, occasionally spooning dressing over tomatoes.

At serving time, drain tomatoes and slice in half, lengthwise. The dressing can be served separately if desired. Place tomatoes in a serving dish and sprinkle the tops with additional parsley.

Serves 8

SWEET AND SOUR ASIAN CUCUMBERS

Ingredients

2 small cucumbers

1 teaspoon salt

1 teaspoon sugar

1 teaspoon rice wine vinegar

1 teaspoon soy sauce

1 teaspoon Thai hot sauce (like Sriracha) or chili oil

Sesame oil

Directions

Peel, seed and cube the cucumbers into bite size pieces and put in a bowl. Sprinkle the salt over them, and let them sit for ½ hour, then drain any excess water out of the bowl.

Add the sugar, vinegar, soy sauce, and hot sauce. Right before serving, splash with the sesame oil.

Serves 4

WATERMELON AND ARUGULA SALAD

Ingredients

⅓ cup thinly sliced red onion

Ice cubes

½ pound seedless watermelon flesh cut into 1-inch chunks (about 2 cups)

2 tablespoons balsamic vinegar

1 tablespoon extra virgin olive oil

Salt and freshly ground pepper

2 6-ounce bunches arugula, stems discarded

¼ cup crumbled goat cheese

Directions

In a small bowl, cover the onion with cold water and ice cubes. Let stand for 30 minutes, the drain and pat dry.

While the onions are soaking, toss the watermelon with 1 tablespoon vinegar and let stand 10 minutes. Whisk the remaining 1 tablespoon vinegar with olive oil and season with salt and pepper. In a bowl, combine the arugula with the onion and add the oil and vinegar mixture, toss gently. Using a slotted spoon, scatter watermelon over the salad and top with cheese.

Serves 2

El Jardin, Carrollton School

JACQUELINE'S STRAWBERRY SPINACH SALAD

Even my children love this salad!!! I make the dressing and adjust the ingredients for individual portions because they will eat it everyday!

Ingredients

2 bags baby spinach leaves

3 small baskets of strawberries

1½ cups slivered almonds

Directions

Cut the strawberries and mix all ingredients in a salad bowl. Pour the dressing over the salad and toss.

Serves 4 to 6

Poppy Seed Dressing

¼ cup sugar

2 tablespoons poppy seeds

¼ cup Worcestershire sauce

¼ cup cider vinegar

Directions

Mix all the ingredients together, cover and set aside.

ROASTED PINEAPPLE AND AVOCADO SALAD

Ingredients

1 pound peeled and cored
fresh pineapple,
cut into ¾ inch chunks

½ teaspoon light brown sugar

Kosher salt, to taste

1½ tablespoons
extra virgin olive oil

1½ tablespoons
balsamic vinegar

2 Hass avocados,
cut into ¾ inch chunks

4 ounces baby spinach
(about 4 cups)

12 mint leaves

Freshly ground pepper

Lime wedges, for serving

Directions

Preheat oven to 400 degrees. In a medium bowl, toss the pineapple with the brown sugar and ½ teaspoon of salt. Spread the pineapple on a baking sheet and roast in the upper third of the oven for about 10 minutes, or until softened and just beginning to brown.

In a medium bowl, whisk the olive oil with the vinegar. Add the avocados, spinach and mint, season with salt and pepper and toss. Transfer the salad to plates, top with the pineapple and serve with lime wedges.

Makes 4 servings

El Jardin

CURRIED SPINACH SALAD

Ingredients

10 ounces fresh spinach, torn in pieces

1½ cups thinly sliced apples

½ cup golden raisins

½ cup peanuts

2 tablespoons sliced scallions

Directions

In a large salad bowl, combine the spinach, apples, raisins, peanuts, and scallions. Shake dressing. Pour over salad and toss.

Serves 4 to 6

Mango Chutney Dressing

¼ cup white wine vinegar

¼ cup vegetable oil

2 tablespoons Villager mango chutney

2 teaspoons sugar

½ teaspoon salt

1½ teaspoons curry powder

1 teaspoon dry mustard

Directions

In a jar with a tight-fitting lid, combine all dressing ingredients. Mix well. Cover and chill.

NUTTY DUCK BREAST SALAD

Make the salad first and chill while you are preparing the duck breasts.

Ingredients

1 bag mixed field greens washed and spun dry

1 Belgian endive, washed and sliced across the length

1 cup shelled walnut or pecan halves

¾ cups dried cranberries

Prepared balsamic vinegar or Annie's Shitake Sesame Vinaigrette Dressing.

Directions

Toss the ingredients together in large salad bowl and sprinkle with the dressing. Refrigerate while you cook the duck.

To serve, arrange the salad on 4 plates and top with the slices of duck breast. Serve with a Pinot Noir or a chilled French Chablis. For those who won't eat "red/raw duck", let the meat rest for 5 minutes before carving, but do not cook more or the meat will turn tough.

Serves 4

Duck

4 duck breasts

Olive oil

Salt and pepper to taste

Directions

Pull any pinfeathers on the duck breasts, wash and pat dry. Score the fatty side with a sharp knife at the diagonal 4-5 times, then cross score diagonally to form Xs.

Rub with olive oil, salt and pepper and place breasts, fat side down, under the broiler for 7 minutes. With a spatula, NOT A FORK, flip breasts, without piercing the meat, and cook 7 minutes more. Thinly slice the breasts, fat side down and at a diagonal. The meat should be slightly pinkish-red.

SALMON NIÇOISE

Ingredients

½ pound green beans, trimmed

6 6-ounce fillets fresh salmon

6 cups assorted greens, trimmed, washed, and dried

Salt and lemon pepper

3 hard boiled eggs, peeled and cut into quarters

12 boiled or steamed red potatoes, or fingerling, or other small potatoes

1 cup pitted Niçoise or Kalamata olives

3 ripe tomatoes, cored, seeded, and cut into quarters

1 yellow bell pepper, stemmed, cut into thin strips

6 anchovies, optional

1 teaspoon capers optional

1 tablespoon chopped fresh chives, optional

Directions

Steam the green beans until tender but still crisp, about 4 minutes. Drain and dip in ice water and drain again. Lightly oil or spray a sauté pan big enough to hold the salmon. Season the salmon with salt and lemon pepper. Cover with a lid and place the cold pan over low heat. Cook about 4 minutes, turn when the sides of the fish turn pale, and cook about 4 minutes on the other side. Remove pan from the heat.

Arrange the greens on a plate, place the salmon in the center, and arrange the other ingredients around. Drizzle dressing over the salad to taste.

Serves 6

Lemon Dressing

2 tablespoons Dijon mustard

2 tablespoons Champagne vinegar

½ teaspoon salt

½ teaspoon garlic pepper, optional

3 tablespoons lemon olive oil

3 tablespoons extra virgin olive oil

Directions

To make the dressing, mix the mustard, vinegar, salt and pepper together. Whisk in the olive oils until emulsified. Cover and set aside.

MANGO CHUTNEY CHICKEN SALAD

I love to tweak recipes where I can sneak in some
of our famous Villager mango chutney!

Ingredients

½ cup mayonnaise

½ cup sour cream

1 tablespoon
Durkey's Famous Dressing

½ teaspoon curry

1 heaping teaspoon
Villager mango chutney

Salt and pepper to taste

4 cups cooked chicken, cubed

2 cups diced celery

1 cup seedless green grapes,
halved

½ cup toasted slivered almonds
(optional)

Directions

Combine the mayonnaise, sour cream, Durkey's famous dressing, curry, mango chutney, salt and pepper. Add the rest of the ingredients. Chill before serving.

Serves 8

HOMEMADE CAESAR DRESSING

A secret recipe that leaves out the anchovies, but you would never know it! The crumbled blue cheese makes it taste just like the original.

Ingredients

½ cup extra virgin olive oil

1 egg

2 garlic cloves, crushed

2 tablespoons fresh lemon juice

½ teaspoon salt

½ teaspoon pepper

1 teaspoon Worcestershire sauce

¼ cup crumbled blue cheese

½ cup grated Parmesan cheese

Directions

Combine all the ingredients in a blender until creamy. This makes enough to serve 4 to 6 people. Toss with romaine or your favorite greens.

Makes about 1 ½ cups of dressing

GREEN BEAN, BEET, AND FETA SALAD

Ingredients

2 pounds fresh green beans, ends trimmed

2 pounds baby beets in a glass jar, not canned

¾ cup plus 2 tablespoons extra-virgin olive oil

¾ cup red wine vinegar

Salt and freshly ground pepper

4 shallots, thinly sliced

¾ cup chopped fresh basil,

8 ounces feta or goat cheese, crumbled

1 tablespoon fresh mint, chopped

Directions

Steam the green beans 2 to 5 minutes, until crisp tender. Rinse in cold water and drain well.

In a serving bowl whisk the oil and vinegar. Add salt and pepper to taste. Add all the ingredients, toss to coat, and then serve.

Serves 8

CURRIED TUNA SALAD

A dazzling mix of subtle flavors... not your typical tuna salad!

Ingredients

2 7-ounce packages of chunk light tuna

1 tablespoon curry

1 tablespoon Gulden's spicy brown mustard, no substitutions

2 tablespoons mayonnaise, or to taste

¼ cup golden raisins

¼ cup dried cranberries

Splash of white wine

Salt and fresh ground pepper to taste

1 scallion, sliced thin, including green part

Assorted greens such as arugula, watercress, and romaine

Lemon salad dressing (see page 66)

½ ripe cantaloupe

1 red apple, cored

Directions

Drain the tuna and add the curry and mustard. Add a splash of white wine to moisten the tuna. The amount of wine will depend upon how dry the tuna is. Then add 1 teaspoon of mayonnaise at a time to reach desired consistency.

Stir in the raisins and cranberries . Season with salt and pepper.

Toss the greens with enough lemon salad dressing to coat. Cut the rind off the cantaloupe and cut into bite size pieces or slices. Cut the apple into bite size pieces or slices. Toss the cantaloupe and apple with some of the dressing.

Arrange greens on individual plates. Place a large serving spoon of tuna mixture in the center. Arrange the cantaloupe and apple around the tuna. Sprinkle the scallion over each of the salads.

Serves 4

MADE WITH LOVE

Villager Breads, Chutneys & Quilts

"In 1998, the Villagers awarded a large grant to the Housekeeper's Club (now the Coconut Grove Women's Club) to replicate the historic windows."

THE VILLAGERS

APPLE PECAN BREAD

Ingredients

2 eggs

1 cup oil

1 cup granulated sugar

½ cup brown sugar

1 teaspoon vanilla

2 cups flour

1 teaspoon salt

1 teaspoon baking soda

1 teaspoon cinnamon

½ cup walnuts or pecans

½ cup raisins, optional

2 Granny Smith apples, peeled, cored and diced

Directions

Preheat oven to 350 degrees. Grease a Bundt pan or a large loaf pan.

Stir by hand. Mix the eggs, oil, granulated sugar, brown sugar and vanilla. Add the flour, salt, baking soda and cinnamon. Stir in the pecans, raisins (if using) and apples.

Bake for an hour or until a toothpick comes out clean.

Makes 1 loaf

Ocean Waves, 1991-92

BRAN MUFFINS

This recipe makes quite a few muffins. The batter can be kept in the fridge for quite a long time, allowing you to bake them in smaller batches, as you need them.

Ingredients

4 beaten eggs

3 cups sugar

1 cup salad oil

1 quart buttermilk

1 15-ounce box raisin bran cereal

2½ cups all-purpose flour

2½ cups whole-wheat flour

1½ teaspoons salt

5 teaspoons baking soda

Directions

Preheat oven to 400 degrees. Combine all the ingredients. Cover and refrigerate.

When ready to bake, put in muffin tins and bake for 15 minutes.

Makes approximately 40 muffins

CRANBERRY BREAD

Ingredients

1 cup fresh cranberries

2 eggs, well beaten

1 cup sugar

1 teaspoon salt

½ cup vegetable oil

1½ cups flour, sifted

1 teaspoon baking soda

Directions

Preheat oven to 350 degrees.
Grease a 5 x 9-inch loaf pan.

Chop the fresh cranberries in a Cuisinart. Add the sugar and eggs, blend until it's pureed. Add the dry ingredients and oil. Pour into a loaf pan and bake for one hour until a toothpick comes out of the center clean.

Makes 1 loaf

BEST WHOLE WHEAT BANANA NUT BREAD

Incredibly healthy!

Ingredients

½ cup cooking oil

1 cup sugar, or ¾ cup if you like

2 eggs beaten

3 ripe bananas mashed

1 cup whole-wheat flour

1 cup unbleached white flour

¼ cup flaxseed meal

1 teaspoon baking soda

½ teaspoon baking powder

½ teaspoon salt

3 tablespoons milk

½ teaspoon vanilla

1 cup chopped nuts,
any variety, optional

Directions

Preheat oven to 350 degrees. Grease and flour a 9 x 5 x 3-inch loaf pan

Beat oil and sugar together, add eggs and banana and beat well. Add dry ingredients, milk and vanilla, and mix well. Stir in nuts, if using.

Pour into the loaf pan, and bake for about 1 hour. Cool and store overnight to allow the flavors to intensify.

Makes 1 loaf

CHEDDAR CORN BREAD

Ingredients

1½ 12-ounce boxes Martha White Yellow Corn Muffin Mix

2 eggs

1 8-ounce can creamed corn

½ cup vegetable oil

1 cup sour cream

Pinch of cayenne pepper

4 ounces shredded sharp cheddar cheese

Directions

Preheat oven to 350 degrees. Mix first 6 ingredients together. Put half of batter in a glass pie plate. Sprinkle on cheddar cheese. Top with the rest of the batter.

Bake for 35 to 40 minutes. Check with a toothpick. It should not be moist in the middle. The top should be light golden brown.

Makes 6 servings

BUTTERMILK BISCUITS

This recipe is a favorite of Emily Savage, the Villager's first President.

Ingredients

2 cups sifted enriched flour

1 tablespoon baking powder

½ teaspoon salt

¼ teaspoon soda

5 tablespoons shortening

1 cup buttermilk

Directions

Preheat oven to 450 degrees. Sift flour, baking powder, salt and soda; cut in shortening until mixture resembles coarse crumbs. Add buttermilk, all at once, and stir until dough follows fork around bowl.

Turn out on board and knead for ½ minute. Roll dough ⅜-inch thick. Brush with melted fat or salad oil. Fold over and cut double biscuits.

Bake on un-greased cookie sheet for 12 to 15 minutes.

Makes about 10 biscuits

Dade County Christmas Pine, 1993-94

DRIED FRUIT MUFFINS

Delicious muffins that don't contain flour.

Ingredients

3 eggs or equivalent Egg Beaters

1 cup raisins

1 cup chopped walnuts

¾ cup chopped dates

⅓ cup sugar or Splenda

Directions

Preheat oven to 350 degrees. Grease mini-muffin pans with Pam or other cooking spray. Mix ingredients and pour into each cup to ½ full. Bake for 10 to 25 minutes.

Makes 2-dozen mini-muffins

RUM BANANA BREAD

Ingredients

¾ cup craisins

3 tablespoons dark rum

1½ cups flour

2 teaspoons baking powder

½ teaspoon baking soda

¼ teaspoon salt

1 teaspoon cinnamon

½ cup unsalted butter, melted

¼ cup packed brown sugar

½ cup sugar

2 eggs

3 very ripe mashed bananas

1 teaspoon vanilla

¾ cup coarsely chopped pecans (optional)

Directions

One hour in advance, bring craisins and the rum to a rapid boil in a small saucepan. Remove from heat, cover and let stand; the craisins should absorb most of the rum.

Preheat oven to 325 degrees. Grease and flour a 9 x 5 x 3-inch pan. Whisk together the flour, baking powder, baking soda, salt and cinnamon.

In a separate bowl, beat the butter with both sugars until fluffy. Beat in eggs one at a time, then the bananas and vanilla. Add the flour mixture and stir just enough to blend; fold in the craisins and pecans (if using).

Spoon the batter into the pan and bake for 50 minutes. Cool on a wire rack.

Makes 1 loaf

HARVEST BREAD

This is a recipe that's been perfected over the years.
The glaze is optional but highly recommended.

Ingredients

3 cups flour, sifted

2 cups sugar

1 teaspoon salt

1 teaspoon baking soda

1 teaspoon ground cinnamon

1 8-ounce can crushed
pineapple with juice
(reserve juice for glaze)

3 eggs, beaten well

1 cup cooking oil

2 cups about 3 bananas, chopped

½ cup chopped walnuts
or pecans (optional)

1½ teaspoons vanilla

Directions

Preheat oven to 325 degrees. Generously grease
two 9 x 5 x 3-inch loaf pans.

Combine all ingredients for bread and stir until
blended. Pour into the prepared pans. Bake for 1 hour
and 10 minutes or until toothpick comes out clean.

Cool in pans for 15 minutes. Remove loaves from
pans and cool completely.

To make the glaze

Combine 1 tablespoon melted butter, 1 cup sifted
powder sugar, 2 tablespoons pineapple juice.
Drizzle over the bread.

Makes 2 loaves

El Jardin's Jewels, 1995-96

DILL MINI-MUFFINS

Ingredients

1 cup butter, softened

1 8-ounce container sour cream

2 cups self-rising flour

1 tablespoon dill seed

2 tablespoons
dried parsley flakes

¼ teaspoon onion powder

Directions

Preheat oven to 375 degrees. Grease 1½ mini-muffin pans. Beat softened butter at medium speed with an electric mixer until creamy; add sour cream, and beat at low speed until blended.

In a separate bowl, combine flour and next 3 ingredients. Stir flour mixture into the butter mixture until blended. Spoon dough into prepared pans. Bake for 15 to 17 minutes, or until golden.

Makes 3 dozen

House Tour, 1996-97

ORANGE BREAD

Ingredients

1 large orange

1 cup raisins or dates

1 teaspoon baking soda

1 cup sugar

2 tablespoons butter

1 egg, beaten

1 teaspoon vanilla

2 cups sifted flour

1 teaspoon baking powder

½ teaspoon salt

½ cup chopped nuts, optional

Directions

Preheat oven to 350 degrees.
Grease a 9 x 5 x 3 inch loaf pan.

Squeeze a large orange and put the juice into a measuring cup. Add hot water to the measuring cup to fill it up until it measures 1 cup. Put the orange rind through a food processor, and measure out 1 cup into a bowl. Discard the rest of the rind.

Add the raisins or dates to the bowl, add baking soda and pour the hot juice over it. Add sugar, butter, beaten egg, vanilla, flour, baking powder and salt. Mix well. Add chopped nuts if desired and mix well.

Bake for 50 minutes, or until done.

Makes 1 loaf

Mariner's Compass, 1998-99

SARAH'S PUMPKIN BREAD

This is my daughter-in-law's family recipe from Houston, Texas.
It's so yummy that everyone always asks her for it!

Ingredients

3½ cups flour, sifted

2 teaspoons baking soda

3 cups sugar

1½ teaspoon salt

2 teaspoons cinnamon

½ teaspoon cloves

1 teaspoon nutmeg

1 cup vegetable oil

4 eggs

⅔ cups water

2 cups canned pumpkin

Directions

Preheat oven to 350 degrees.
Generously grease two 9 x 5 x 3-inch loaf pans.

Sift all dry ingredients into a large bowl and mix well. Add all the other ingredients and mix. Pour into the prepared pans.

Bake for 1 hour or until done. Cool on rack in pans, and then turn on racks to finish cooling. If making muffins, bake for about 20 minutes.

Makes 2 loaves

CRANBERRY CHUTNEY

Ingredients

4 cups fresh cranberries

2 cups packed brown sugar

1 cup raisins

1 cup water

½ cup slivered almonds, toasted

¼ cup fresh lemon juice

¾ teaspoon salt

1 teaspoon grated onion

⅛ teaspoon cloves

Directions

Combine all ingredients in a large saucepan, and bring to a boil. Reduce heat and simmer 20 to 30 minutes, or until thickened. Follow canning instructions on page 91.

Yields 3 ½ to 5 cups

STRAWBERRY BREAD

The strawberry flavor is wonderfully subtle and refreshing!
This bread will freeze nicely.

Ingredients

2 cups fresh strawberries, cleaned, hulled, chopped

4 eggs

1¼ cups oil

3 cups all-purpose flour

1 teaspoon baking soda

1 teaspoon salt

3 teaspoons cinnamon

2 cups sugar

1¼ cups chopped pecans (optional)

Directions

Preheat oven to 350 degrees. Generously grease two 9 x 5 x 3 inch loaf pans.

Mix strawberries, eggs, and oil. Sift dry ingredients together, and mix well with wet ingredients. Gently stir in pecans, if using. Bake in the prepared pans for one hour. Serve with butter or cream cheese.

Makes 2 loaves

Everglades, 2000-01

THE SAVOY LONDON'S TEA SANDWICHES

Minty Egg Sandwich

Hard-boiled eggs

Fresh mint

Mayonnaise

Pepperidge Farm ButterThin Bread

Directions

Chop the eggs with some fresh mint leaves. Mix with a little mayonnaise and place between the bread slices.

Cucumber Tea Sandwich

Cucumbers, sliced

Mayonnaise

Salt and pepper, to taste

Pepperidge Farm Butter Thin Bread

Directions

Spread a little mayonnaise on the bottom slice of the sandwich bread; add salt and pepper to taste. Slice some cucumbers lengthwise and place on top of the mayo. Top with other piece of bread. If using regular sandwich bread, cut off the crust and cut the sandwich into four triangles or squares.

Be generous when you fill each sandwich! Be sure there is at least a ¼ inch or more filling between the slices of bread. A generous amount of filling holds the bread together and makes a prettier presentation!

Chill sandwiches before cutting off the crusts!

Tea sandwiches can be made a day ahead, wrapped in wax paper, and kept in the refrigerator.

ZUCCHINI BREAD

Ingredients

3 eggs

1 cup oil

2 cups sugar

3 cups flour

1 teaspoon salt

½ teaspoon baking powder

1 teaspoon baking soda

2 cups peeled and grated zucchini

3 teaspoons vanilla

¾ teaspoons nutmeg

3 teaspoons cinnamon

1 cup chopped nuts (optional)

Directions

Preheat oven to 350 degrees. Grease and flour two loaf pans.

In a large bowl, mix together the eggs, oil and sugar. In a separate bowl, sift the flour, salt, baking powder and baking soda together and mix well. Add to the wet ingredients. Add the rest of the ingredients, mix well and pour into the loaf pans.

Bake for 1 hour or until toothpick comes out clean.

Makes 2 loaves

Art Deco SoBe, 2001-02

COOKIE'S HOMEMADE GRANOLA

This is a versatile recipe. Add flaxseeds, coconut, or different varieties of nuts.
At holiday time add craisins, cranberries or dried cherries.
All variations are excellent. Makes a great hostess gift.

Ingredients

4 cups old fashioned oats

½ cup wheat germ

¼ cup unsalted sunflower seeds

1 teaspoon cinnamon

½ cup chopped pecans

¼ cup chopped almonds

½ cup brown sugar

1 teaspoon salt, optional

⅓ cup vegetable oil

4 tablespoons honey

½ cup water

1 teaspoon vanilla

1 cup raisins & 1 cup dates

Directions

Preheat oven to 300 degrees. In a large bowl combine first eight ingredients. Mix well.

In another bowl, mix together the oil, honey, water and vanilla. Pour the liquid mixture over the dry ingredients and mix well. Spread over a jellyroll pan sprayed with nonstick spray.

Bake for 50 to 60 minutes. Granola will brown as it cooks. Cool on a wire rack, then, stir in the raisins and dates. Store in an airtight container.

Makes approximately 10 cups

Stiltsville, 2002-03

TUSCAN CORN BREAD

*I prefer to use mini muffin pans for this recipe,
which only requires 10-12 minutes of bake time.*

Ingredients

1 cup flour

1 cup coarse yellow cornmeal

2 tablespoons sugar

4 teaspoons baking powder

¼ teaspoon salt

1 cup milk

⅓ cup grated Parmesan cheese

¼ cup vegetable oil

2 eggs, beaten

1 cup pitted, chopped
Kalamata olives

1 2-ounce jar drained,
chopped pimentos

2 tablespoons snipped
fresh parsley

Directions

Preheat oven 425 degrees. Spray a 9 x 9 inch
baking pan with non-stick spray.

Combine the flour, cornmeal, sugar, baking powder
and salt in bowl and mix well. Stir in the milk,
cheese, oil and eggs. Fold in the olives, pimentos
and parsley. Spoon batter into prepared pan. Bake
20 minutes.

Serves 6 to 8

Stiltsville Wall Hanging, 2003

TOMATO MARMALADE

Ingredients

5 cups prepared tomatoes

1 lemon

2 oranges

4 cups sugar

Directions

To prepare the tomatoes: scald in boiling water for 30 seconds to remove the skins. Cut in half and squeeze out the juice and seeds. Chop the pulp coarsely. You will need 5 cups. Peel oranges and lemon. Slice and remove the seeds. Chop the pulp. Slice the peels into thin strips and set aside. In a pot, combine the tomato, orange and lemon pulp. Boil for 10 minutes.

Add the sliced citrus peel and sugar. Cook over high heat until peel is transparent and marmalade is thick, stirring frequently, about 1½ hours. Ladle into hot sterile jars and follow directions for canning on page 91. Boil for 10 minutes in the jars. Remove from water and cool over night before storing in a cool place.

Yields about 5 (8-ounce) jars

Destination Miami, 2004-05

STAR FRUIT PICKLES

Ingredients

24 carambola (star fruit) cut into ½-inch stars

2 onions

2 sweet red or green peppers

3 large carrots

3 celery stalks

7 cups water

2 cups white vinegar

4 tablespoons salt

3 garlic cloves, quartered and crushed

3 tiny red chili peppers, deseeded and halved

1 tablespoon pickling spice

Directions

Place carambola stars in a large bowl. Cut onions and the sweet peppers into 1-inch pieces and add to the carambola. Cut carrots and celery into 2-inch lengths and add to the mixture. Toss. Heat water, vinegar, and salt to boiling. Keep hot while dividing the star mixture among three (1-quart) sterilized jars. To each jar, add four garlic pieces, 2 pieces of chili pepper, and 1 teaspoon pickling spice.

Pour boiling liquid into sterilized jars and fill to within ⅛-inch of the rim. Close jars and cool. Refrigerate and use within 6 months.

Yields 3 quarts

Calle Ocho, 2006-07

GREEN MANGO CHUTNEY

Hélène Muller Pancoast is the granddaughter of David Fairchild, famed botanist and plant explorer. This is one of her family's favorite chutney recipes.

Ingredients

2 pounds white sugar

1 pound brown sugar

1 liter vinegar

6 pounds green mangos fully mature but hard and green

½ pound raisins

1 pound green papaya, chopped

1 ounce chopped fresh ginger

2 cloves garlic, chopped fine

1 ounce chopped limes, (including rind and juice)

½ teaspoon tamarind pulp

1 ounce red chili pepper

1 teaspoon nutmeg

Directions

Boil together the sugars and vinegar for 45 minutes at a hard boil. This can be left overnight at this point and continued the next day. Peel mangos, slice off the seed and coarsely chop. Add green mangos, raisins, papaya, fresh ginger and garlic. Bring back to a boil and boil hard for approximately 1 hour or until thickened, stirring to keep from burning. Add the rest of the ingredients and cook ½ hour more at a simmer.

If the mixture seems thin, remove a cup of the mixture with mangos and put through a blender. Add towards the end of cooking time as this helps to "jell" the mixture. Turn off stove and let stand for 20-30 minutes. The chutney can be bottled either hot or cold.

10 to 14 ½-pint jars

Note: *be very careful as the mixture can boil over and burn very easily. I use a wide, deep cooking pot, and spray the bottom and sides with plain "Pam" which seems to help the sticking a little.*

SPICED CRANBERRY CHUTNEY

The chutney is better if it is made a few days ahead.
It also freezes well if you don't want to go though the canning process.
Goes beautifully as an accompaniment to pork dishes.

Ingredients

2¼ cups packed brown sugar

1½ cups cranberry juice

½ cup apple cider vinegar

½ teaspoon ground ginger

¼ teaspoon allspice

2 12-oz. bags fresh cranberries

2 oranges, peel and
pith removed, segmented

1 Granny Smith apple, peeled,
cored and chopped

½ cup dried currants

½ cup dried apricots, chopped

2 tbsp. grated orange peel

Directions

Combine first 5 ingredients in large heavy saucepan. Stir over medium heat until sugar dissolves. Increase heat and bring to a boil. Add remaining ingredients and bring back to a boil. Reduce heat and simmer until mixture is thick, stirring frequently, about 40 minutes.
Cool completely.

Yields 8-9 cups

Gifts from the Sea, 2007-08

CHOW-CHOW

Grandma MacDonald came from Scotland in the 1800s and brought this recipe with her. It is unique in that there is no cabbage or peppers in the recipe. It's a great relish that can be used anytime, with any dish that calls for relish.

Ingredients

5 pounds medium green tomatoes, seeded

3 pounds medium Granny Smith apples, cored

2 pounds yellow onions

½ cup salt

2 pounds white sugar

1 quart apple cider vinegar

½ cup pickling spice in a cheesecloth bag

Directions

Cut tomatoes and apples in quarters. Chop onions fine. Mix tomatoes, apples, and onions with salt in a non-reactive bowl.

Cover and leave overnight on the counter. Drain in the morning. Then add sugar, vinegar and the spice bag. Boil for one hour until soft.

Discard the spice bag. If you are canning, process in the water bath for 10 minutes, and follow the canning directions on page 91.

Makes 10 pints

MOTHER HANSON'S MANGO JAM

This was my mother's recipe and we've made it for many years.

Ingredients

13 cups of mangoes, peeled, seeded and cut into slices

1 cup of lemon or lime juice

6½ cups sugar

Directions

Cook mangoes and juice down for about 30 minutes, uncovered. Add sugar and continue to cook on very low heat uncovered until the jam is thick enough to suit you. Stir often so it doesn't stick. I can it in mason jars, processing for 20 minutes after it boils. Keeps indefinitely in refrigerator. It's great on ice cream, as a topping for cheesecake or on toast.

CANNING INSTRUCTIONS

The usual size is ½ pint jars. The jars must be sterilized (in the dishwasher works fine). Both the inner lid of a jar and the product must be hot for the canning process to be successful. Heat the inner lids by boiling them before using.

Fill jars with jam or chutney, leaving ½-inch at top. Be sure the rim of jar is clean. Put on a hot inner lid and screw a rim onto the jar gently. (Never reuse inner lids from old jars, however the outer rims are reusable.)

Place in pot of water that comes just below the level of the lid. When the water comes to a boil, time for 20 minutes, unless a recipe specifies otherwise. Carefully remove the jars from the water with large tongs and cool.

Check jars to be sure the lid is sealed (the lid should be firm and not move). If lid moves it must be re-processed. Throw away the inner lid and process it again with a new inner lid. Canned goods may be stored at room temperature.

Flor-da-lilly, 2008-09

VILLAGER TEA SANDWICHES

Tea sandwiches are one of the mainstays of the Villagers' Home and Garden Tours. The following recipes are delicious — with a minimum of preparation.

Helpful Hints For Making Tea Sandwiches

Choose regular sliced loaves of bread. Thin sliced breads often curl as they sit out on the table. Do not let cream cheese or butter get too soft before mixing. If you use a blender, pulse sparingly and do not over blend. If the cream cheese mixture becomes too soft, place the filling in the refrigerator for 30 minutes before spreading on the sandwiches.

Be generous when you fill each sandwich! Be sure there is at least a ¼ inch or more filling between the slices of bread. A generous amount of filling holds the bread together and makes a prettier presentation! Chill sandwiches before cutting off the crusts! Clean serrated knife blade before cutting the next sandwich.

Tea sandwiches can be made a day ahead, wrapped in wax paper, and kept in the refrigerator. Preparation time takes about two hours for making sandwiches using 36-ounces of cream cheese and 3 to 4 loafs of bread.

If you are making chicken or tuna salad tea sandwiches, spread a thin layer of mayonnaise or butter over both bread faces before filling to keep the sandwich from becoming soggy!

Cucumber Tea Sandwiches

8 ounces cream cheese

½ stick butter

1 cucumber, peeled, seeded, pureed and drained

2 teaspoons onion, minced

2 teaspoons dill weed

Salt to taste

Tabasco to taste, optional

Sprigs of dill, for garnish

¾ loaf of Pepperidge Farm Oatmeal Wheat, or 7 Grain Bread

Directions

Blend the cream cheese, butter, salt, and dill weed. Add cucumber, onion, and Tabasco.

Prepare, chill, trim and garnish with small sprigs of dill.

Makes 12 sandwiches

Olive Tea Sandwiches

1 cup pimento-stuffed
olives, drained

8 ounces cream cheese, softened

¼ to ½ cup milk

¾ cup chopped walnuts
or pecans, optional

¾ loaf of Pepperidge Farm
Oatmeal Wheat or 7 Grain Bread

Directions

Coarsely chop ¾ cup of the pimento-stuffed olives in a Cuisinart (reserving the other ¼ cup olives for garnish). Remove olive mixture from the bowl.

Pulse the cream cheese with just enough milk to make a smooth filling. Add chopped pimento-olives to cream cheese, and nuts if desired. Mix in by hand. If mixture seems too soft, refrigerate for ½ hour before spreading. Prepare, chill and trim as you would the apricot tea sandwiches. Slice the remaining stuffed olives to use as a garnish.

Makes 12 sandwiches

Apricot Tea Sandwiches

8 ounces cream cheese, softened

¼ stick unsalted butter, softened

Pinch of salt

½ cup apricot preserves

4 ounces dried apricots

¾ loaf Pepperidge Farm Wheat
Cinnamon Bread with Raisins

Dried apricots and parsley
for garnish

Directions

Coarsely chop the dried apricots in a Cuisinart. Remove from the Cuisinart. Place cream cheese, butter and salt in the Cuisinart and pulse until smooth. Add apricot preserves and apricots to cream cheese filling, mixing together by hand. If mixture seems too soft, refrigerate for ½ hour before spreading on sandwiches.

Prepare sandwiches by spreading at least ¼ inch of filling between slices of bread. Stack 2 to 3 sandwiches on top of each other, placing them back into the plastic bread wrapper. Repeat until bread bag is filled with sandwiches. Refrigerate for at least an hour.

One at a time, remove sandwiches from wrapper and trim crusts. Cut each sandwich into squares or triangles. Clean knife after cutting each sandwich. Top with a small slice of dried apricot and a bit of parsley leaf. Wrap in wax paper and store in refrigerator until ready to use.

Makes 12 sandwiches. Quadruple the recipe to make 40 sandwiches (uses 3 to 4 loaves of bread.)

PERFECTLY POLITE PASTA

Pasta Dishes

"A variety of Villager grants over the years have allowed the
original Coconut Grove Schoolhouse to get a new roof,
landscaping and a memorabilia display."

JACK'S BAKED ZITI

Ingredients

½ pound ziti pasta

1 pound ricotta cheese

3 cups shredded mozzarella cheese

3 cups prepared spaghetti sauce

½ cups grated Parmesan cheese

Directions

Preheat oven to 350 degrees. Cook ziti in boiling water 9 minutes. Place in a large bowl. Combine ricotta and ½ of mozzarella cheese. Add to ziti and mix.

Grease a 9 x 13 x 2-inch baking dish. Put ½ of the spaghetti sauce on bottom of the dish. Spoon the ziti mixture on top. Cover with remaining sauce. Put Parmesan and remaining mozzarella cheese on top. Bake 20-30 minutes. Let stand 20 minutes before serving.

Serves 8 to 10

SCALLOP PASTA

with Saffron Sauce

Ingredients

2 pinches saffron threads or powder

6 tablespoons hot water

4 shallots, minced

6 cloves garlic, minced

2 tablespoons butter or olive oil

½ cup dry white wine

2 cups heavy cream

4 medium roasted red and yellow peppers, peeled, julienned

3 leeks, white part only, julienned

Salt and white pepper to taste

4 cups fettucine, cooked and drained

2 pounds sea scallops, sliced ¼-inch thick

Directions

Soak the saffron thread in the water. Sauté the shallots, and the garlic over low heat in the olive oil or butter. When the shallots and garlic are soft, but not browned, add the wine and raise the heat to medium-high. Reduce the wine until you have about 2 tablespoons liquid.

Gradually whisk in the cream to make the sauce. Cook the sauce until thickened. Add the bell peppers, and stir to heat through. Add the sliced scallops and cook for 3 minutes. Strain the saffron liquid into the sauce. Season to taste with salt and pepper and toss with the pasta.

Serves 4

FARFALLE

with Mascarpone, Asparagus, and Hazelnuts

Ingredients

2 pounds slender asparagus, trimmed and cut on the diagonal into 2-inch pieces

salt and pepper, to taste

3 tablespoons olive oil

1 pound farfalle (bowtie) pasta

1 8-ounce container mascarpone cheese

⅔ cup grated Parmesan cheese

½ cup hazelnuts, toasted, husked, coarsely chopped

Parmesan cheese shavings

red pepper flakes, to taste (optional)

Directions

Preheat oven to 450 degrees. Line rimmed baking sheet with foil. Place the asparagus on the baking sheet. Sprinkle with salt and pepper. Toss with the olive oil to coat and spread it back out in a single layer. Roast until asparagus is tender, probably less than 5 minutes.

Cook pasta until still firm to bite. Drain, reserving 1 cup of the cooking water. Return pasta to pot. Stir in mascarpone, grated Parmesan and asparagus. Toss over medium heat until pasta is coated with sauce and mixture is heated through. Add reserved pasta water by ¼ cupfuls, if dry. Mound the pasta in large shallow bowl. Sprinkle with the hazelnuts, red pepper flakes (if using) and Parmesan cheese shavings.

Serves 4 to 6

SHRIMP CACCIATORE

with Penne Pasta

Ingredients

2 tablespoons olive oil

2 cups thinly sliced
fresh mushrooms

1 cup thinly sliced
green pepper strips

1 medium onion sliced
lengthwise & cut into strips

2 cloves minced garlic

1 28-ounce can whole tomatoes,
un-drained & chopped

1 cup tomato sauce

1 teaspoon dried basil leaves

8 ounces penne or rigatone

¾ pound medium fresh shrimp,
peeled and de-veined

Salt and ground pepper to taste

Directions

In a large saucepan, heat oil at medium heat. Sauté the mushrooms, green pepper, onion, and garlic, stirring frequently, about 5 minutes, or until the vegetables are tender. Add tomatoes with their juice, tomato sauce, and basil and heat to boiling.

Reduce heat and simmer 20 minutes uncovered until the sauce thickens. Meanwhile, cook pasta according to package instructions and drain. Add shrimp to thickened sauce and cook until pink, about 3 minutes. Season to taste; toss hot pasta and sauce.

Serves 4

BROCCOLI PASTA

with Two Cheeses

Ingredients

1 pound penne or ziti

4 tablespoons butter

2 garlic cloves, minced

1 head of broccoli,
bite-size pieces, steamed

1 cup heavy cream

½ cup milk, more if needed

⅓ cup crumbled
goat cheese or cream cheese

¾ cup fresh grated Parmesan
cheese, more for serving

½ cup slivered Proscuitto or ham

Salt and freshly ground
black pepper, to taste

Directions

Cook pasta al dente, drain and rinse under cold
water, and drain again.

In a saucepan, over medium low heat, add butter.
When melted, add garlic and sauté, stirring for
2 minutes. Raise heat to medium high and add
broccoli and drained pasta tossing to coat. Add
cream, milk and goat cheese. Cook, tossing gently
until cream begins to boil and sauce is smooth. Add
the grated Parmesan and ham tossing gently just
until cheese is melted. Season with salt and pepper.

Thin sauce if necessary with a splash of milk and
serve immediately. Serve with extra Parmesan on
the side.

Serves 4 to 6

MANICOTTI

Ingredients

1 pound ground beef or sausage

2 to 3 cloves garlic, minced

1 cup cottage cheese

6 ounces mozzarella

½ teaspoon salt

½ cup mayonnaise

8 ounces manicotti,
cooked and drained

1 16-ounce jar spaghetti sauce

½ teaspoon dried oregano

2 tablespoons Parmesan cheese

Directions

Preheat oven to 325 degrees. Brown the meat
with the garlic. Mix together the cottage cheese,
mozzarella, salt and mayonnaise. Add to the meat
mixture.

Fill the noodles with the meat/cheese mixture, and
place in a buttered casserole dish. Put the spaghetti
sauce on top, sprinkle with oregano and Parmesan
cheese. Bake for 10 minutes covered, then uncover
and bake an additional ten minutes.

Serves 4

SUMMER LINGUINE

with Tomatoes and Basil

A delicious and easy uncooked pasta sauce to serve during those sultry summer days. To make this for a buffet, substitute large tomatoes with cherry tomatoes, cut in half, and use shell pasta instead of the linguine.

Ingredients

**4 ripe large tomatoes
cut into ½ inch cubes**

**1 pound Brie cheese,
rind removed,
torn into irregular pieces**

**1 cup cleaned fresh basil leaves,
cut into strips**

**3 garlic cloves,
peeled and finely minced**

1 cup extra virgin olive oil

**½ teaspoon freshly ground
black pepper**

2½ teaspoons salt

1 ½ pounds linguine

Freshly grated Parmesan cheese

Directions

Combine tomatoes, Brie, basil, garlic, olive oil, ½ teaspoon salt and pepper in large serving bowl. Prepare at least 2 hours before serving and set aside, covered at room temperature, to let the flavors meld.

Bring 6 quarts water to boil in large pot. Add salt and linguine and boil until tender but still firm, 8 to 10 minutes.

Drain pasta and immediately toss with the sauce. Serve at once with grated Parmesan cheese.

Serves 4 to 6

BLACK MUSSELS

with Linguini

Ingredients

3 tablespoons
extra virgin olive oil

½ white onion, thinly sliced

3 cloves garlic, thinly sliced

1 teaspoon red pepper flakes
or less as desired

4 anchovy fillets,
washed and dried

3 pounds black mussels, cleaned

1¼ cups dry white wine

¼ cup Italian parsley leaves,
snipped with scissors to
a medium fine consistency

1 pound thin linguini

Directions

Bring a covered stockpot of water to boil
and salt to taste.

Meanwhile, in another deep saucepan or stockpot,
sauté the white onions in the olive oil until
translucent. Add the garlic and red pepper flakes
to the onion and cook, without coloring,
on low heat for a few minutes. Add anchovies
and mash until dissolved.

Add pasta to the salted boiling water pot at this
time. Add the mussels and white wine to the onion
mixture and cover the pot. Steam until mussels
are open and flesh is cooked (do not over cook the
mussels). Add snipped parsley to the mussels in the
last minute of cooking. Cook pasta until al dente,
strain, and mix with mussels and wine sauce. Let sit
two minutes to absorb the flavors and serve.

Serves 6

SPAGHETTI

with Chickpea Sauce

The unusual flavor of this sauce comes from the rosemary. It provides a welcome change from the "traditional" Italian seasonings used in pasta dishes. Since canned chickpeas and Parmesan contain ample salt, the sauce doesn't need any extra. The sauce can be prepared while the pasta cooks, or it can be made ahead and reheated when you are ready to cook the pasta.

Ingredients

2 15-ounce cans chickpeas, kept separate, not drained

2 tablespoons olive oil

4 large cloves garlic, minced, about 4 teaspoons

1½ cups thinly sliced onions

1 16-ounce can tomatoes, drained and cut up, with liquid reserved

1 teaspoon crushed rosemary

¼ cup minced fresh parsley

Freshly ground black pepper to taste

1 pound spaghetti, cooked and drained

¼ cup grated Parmesan

Directions

In a blender or food processor, puree 1 can of the chickpeas with its liquid.

In a large saucepan, heat the oil and sauté the garlic and onions until the garlic begins to brown. Add the tomatoes and their liquid, rosemary, chickpea puree, and the remaining can of whole chickpeas with its liquid to the saucepan.
Stir often, heat the mixture for about 15 minutes or until it has thickened. Add the parsley and fresh ground pepper.

Toss the hot cooked spaghetti with the sauce and sprinkle it with the Parmesan before serving.

Serves 6

FLUTED SHELLS

with Spicy Carrot Sauce

Prep time may seem a little long with dicing the vegetables, but the effort is well worth it. The wonderful sweet/spicy flavor will surprise and please guests.

Ingredients

8 ounces carrots, peeled and finely chopped

1 stick celery, finely chopped

4 garlic cloves, finely chopped

¼ teaspoon crushed red pepper flakes

1 tablespoon dried thyme

16 ounces unsalted chicken or vegetable stock, divided in half

4 tablespoons red wine vinegar

½ ounce unsalted butter

¼ teaspoon salt

Freshly ground pepper

8 ounces shell-shaped pasta

1½ teaspoons salt

Directions

Put the carrots, celery, garlic, red pepper flakes, thyme and enough stock to cover them in a saucepan. Bring the mixture to a boil, then cover and reduce the heat to medium. Simmer the vegetables until they are tender, about 20 minutes. Pour 8 ounces of the stock into the carrot mixture and cook until the liquid is reduced to approximately 4 tablespoons, about 20 minutes more. Stir in the butter, salt, and pepper into the sauce.

While you are reducing the second portion of stock, cook the pasta in 5 pints of boiling water with 1½ teaspoons of salt. Start testing the pasta after 5 minutes and cook it until it is al dente. Drain the pasta, put it in a bowl, and toss it with the sauce.

Serves 6

103

JERK CHICKEN

Penne Pasta

This original recipe is compliments of Cindy Hutson, owner/executive chef of Ortanique, Cuisine of the Sun, in Coral Gables, Florida.

Penne Pasta

1 tablespoon herb butter (sweet butter mixed with salt, pepper, chopped parsley, thyme)

1½ pounds marinated julienned chicken

1 pound shitake mushrooms or any mushroom, sliced

4 ounces sun dried tomatoes, sliced

2 ounces fresh basil, chopped

½ Knorr Swiss bouillon cube

1 teaspoon black pepper

2 cups heavy cream

1 pound cooked penne pasta

Directions

Place herbed butter in a sauté pan, and add the rest of the ingredients except the heavy cream and sauté. When chicken is ½ way cooked, add heavy cream and reduce until the sauce is thick and creamy. Take care not to let the sauce separate. Toss with the cooked penne pasta.

Serves 4

Jerk Marinade

1½ pounds julienned chicken breast

5 garlic cloves crushed

¼ cup sesame oil

½ cup teriyaki

¼ cup Busha Browne jerk paste, or other brand

Directions

Put all jerk ingredients in a bowl and marinate chicken for 1-2 hours. You may marinate overnight for a stronger jerk taste.

SPAGHETTI CARBONARA

Ingredients

6 ounces bacon

4 ounces spaghetti or linguine

1 large egg yolk

2 tablespoons heavy whipping cream

Variations

- Add a small chopped onion to the bacon while frying.

- Use fettuccini instead of spaghetti.

- Add ½ cup of shredded Parmesan cheese to the egg yolk and whipping cream when mixing.

Directions

Cook the bacon until crisp in a frying pan. Meanwhile, cook the spaghetti or linguine. In a bowl, whisk a large egg yolk with the heavy whipping cream.

To assemble, remove bacon from the pan and mop up some of the excess bacon fat with a paper towel. Crumble the bacon and return to the pan. Put the frying pan back on a low heat and add the drained pasta to the crispy bacon. Stir it around to capture all the flavor of the bacon. Still on a gentle heat, add the egg and cream and stir evenly. Serve immediately.

Serves 2

Water pump at the old schoolhouse

NORCINA

Ingredients

1½ pounds hot or mild Italian sausage, or 1 or 2 per person

1 onion, chopped

3 garlic cloves, minced

1 cup heavy cream

⅓ cup dry white wine

½ teaspoon salt

½ teaspoon freshly ground black pepper or red pepper

¼ cup chopped fresh parsley

1 pound rigatoni

¾ cup grated Parmagiano Reggiano

Directions

Remove skins from hot Italian sausages. Cut sausage into bite size pieces. In a skillet, sauté garlic and chopped onion in olive oil. Before garlic and onion turn brown, add sausage and some white wine (do not float or boil sausage). Let sausage cook on the bottom of the pan.

Bring the mixture almost to a boil, and begin to add heavy whipping cream a little at a time until the sauce becomes creamy. Add about ½ wine and taste. You may only need to add ½ of the wine and ½ of the whipping cream. Vary proportions to taste. Stir as necessary.

Add red pepper, or coarsely ground black pepper, and salt to taste. Add the chopped parsley. Cook rigatoni pasta until al dente. Drain and return to the cooking pot. Pour Norcina sauce over pasta and add ½ cup Parmagiano Reggiano. Mix with a wooden spoon. Dust with course ground black pepper and serve. Serve the remaining ¼ cup of Parmagiano Reggiano on the side.

Serves 4

PENNE

with Vodka Cream Sauce

The following is one of the Munday family's favorite pasta dishes.

Ingredients

2 tablespoons olive oil

1 small onion, chopped

3 cloves minced fresh garlic

1 28-ounce can crushed tomatoes

¾ teaspoon thyme

¾ teaspoon oregano

½ teaspoon dried red chili flakes

⅓ cup low-salt canned chicken or vegetable broth

⅓ cup Vodka

1 pound cooked mild or hot sausage, or a combination of both, optional

½ cup heavy cream

¼ cup freshly grated Parmesan cheese

¼ cup chopped fresh flat-leaf parsley, optional

8 ounces penne pasta, cooked and drained

Directions

Sauté onion and garlic in olive oil until limp. Add tomatoes, herbs, chili flakes, chicken broth, vodka, and sausage. Cover, and let simmer for 30 minutes, stirring often.

Add more broth if the sauce is too thick. Add heavy cream and reduce for a few minutes. Under-reducing it will result in a soupy sauce. Over-reducing may cause the cream to break. Serve the sauce over pasta, sprinkle with Parmesan and parsley. The sauce freezes well.

Serves 4

*The frame vernacular house that
Mariah Brown built, circa 1890*

Mariah Brown

Born in 1851 at the Bogue, Eleuthera, Mariah left the impoverished Bahamas to live and work in the thriving city of Key West, determined to build a better life for her family. She appeared on the 1885 Key West Census as Maria Hall along with her children Olivia E., Lula and Alice. Charles and Isabella Peacock searched Key West to find someone with a pioneer spirit like their own, to work at their hotel in Coconut Grove. They found "Mary the Washerwoman," who packed up her three girls and journeyed to the South Florida wilderness.

Undaunted by alligators, rattlesnakes, panthers and bears, Mariah labored long days at the Inn and invited her Bahamian friends to "yuk up" their courage and join her. They cleared mangroves and planted in the rocky soil all manner of fruit trees and flowering bushes brought from the Bahamas. From the vantage point of the Peacock Inn, the hub of the growing pioneer community, Mariah worked alongside the women of the Housekeepers Club (now the Coconut Grove Women's Club) to improve the quality of life of their neighbors.

Mariah bought land west of the main road (Charles Avenue) and built a house so strong that it would be there long after she was gone. Other families followed suit. The little settlement, now called Village West, grew to include workers from America's South. Together they planned ways to raise money to improve their community. Mariah probably sold batches of almond candy to raise the money needed to build a church, a school and a library. In 1892 she married Ernest Brown.

Across the river, the instant incorporation of the city of Miami in 1896 brought social conflict, soon aggravated to a violent pitch by the arrival of soldiers preparing to fight in the Spanish-American War. Mariah kept her daughters safe in her Coconut Grove home until they married. Their children thrived as Mariah tended her garden, burying the seeds of generosity and kindness deep in community life.

In the scant documented information about Mariah Brown's life, one detail supported a personal story. The 1885 Key West Census stated that Mariah could not read. The 1900 Coconut Grove Census stated that she could read. How did a woman with three children and a blind husband, a woman working a 14-hour day, find the time and energy to learn to read? As she lived her life, she doubtless tackled the challenge with passion, humor, courage and joy. In the solo play *Mariah Brown*, as Mariah read Walt Whitman's Song of Myself she said, "His words fairly eat ya up." A celebration of her life is a celebration of South Florida communities.

— Dr. Sandra Riley

Mariah Brown's Almond Candy Recipe

If asked for her Bahamian Almond Candy Recipe, Mariah would say:

"Cut open de seeds, chop up and boil down de nuts wid some sugar, den throw a lil' coc'nut in dere. Hum. Good."

Villa Serena was designated a historic site in 2007 by the City of Miami.

William Jennings Bryan

William Jennings Bryan, the Democratic Party's candidate for president on three occasions, was early Miami's most famous resident. A Nebraskan, Bryan and his wife, Mary Baird Bryan, chose the temperate climes of Miami for their winter home in 1912. They had purchased from land-rich Mary Brickell a large wooded lot between the shoreline of Biscayne Bay and beautiful Brickell Avenue (on a stretch known as Millionaire's Row) as the site of their home.

Villa Serena, a large, splendid Mediterranean style home, arose there in subsequent months. It quickly became a gathering place for the public whom Bryan, beloved as a Populist leader, addressed on a variety of topics from his balcony overlooking the tranquil waters of Biscayne Bay. The estate was a virtual environmental farm, with over 80 varieties of trees and flowering shrubs. Bryan had a fondness for radishes, so he planted and tended to several patches around the house.

Miamians loved the unpretentious Bryan, who dove into the city's social, religious, and civic swirl. They sought his opinion on a number of issues while requesting his assistance for various causes. Locals would offer him inviting jobs and opportunities. Bryan's superb oratory gifts served him well when he began delivering Biblical addresses to large crowds in the First Presbyterian Church in downtown Miami and, later, in nearby Royal Palm Park.

Following his resignation, in 1915, as Secretary of State in the administration of President Woodrow Wilson, Bryan made Miami his permanent home. In subsequent years, he played a deeper role in community affairs while maintaining a keen interest in national and international issues and events. At Villa Serena he welcomed a bevy of prominent visitors, including President Warren G. Harding, Premier Eleutherios Venizelos of Greece, and designer Louis Comfort Tiffany.

In 1924, the Bryans moved from Villa Serena to Marymount, a beautiful home near Biscayne Bay in Coconut Grove. In the same year, Bryan accepted a lavish offer from George E. Merrick, the visionary developer of Coral Gables, to promote that community. Throughout the early months of 1925, while Miami's great real estate boom was reaching its peak, Bryan regaled prospective purchasers of real estate from a raft in beautiful Venetian Pool on the uniqueness of southeast Florida and the importance of owning property in Coral Gables.

A few months later in July 1925, he would die from heart failure, just a few days after completing the famous "Scopes Monkey Trial." What is amazing is the fact that Bryan lived as long as he did, for his appetite was prodigious and eclectic. One day on the campaign trail in 1896, a reporter observed the young candidate's breakfast and related it in an article. Bryan, he observed, ate six eggs, one-half of a ham, a half loaf of toasted bread and a full plate of pancakes swimming in butter and syrup. He then washed down the whole sumptuous meal with a pot of coffee!

— *Dr. Paul S. George*

Charles Deering's estate included the 1896 Richmond Cottage, and the Stone House which he built in 1922.

Charles Deering

Charles Deering (1852-1927) was the older half-brother to James Deering of Villa Vizcaya in Coconut Grove. He was a wealthy Chicago industrialist and, like James, was an art dealer and early environmentalist. But unlike his brother, who adored ornate surroundings and lavish parties, Charles preferred austere architecture and low-key celebrations with family.

Charles grew up during the Civil War and was fascinated by it. He knew early in life that he wanted a naval career and graduated second in his class from the Naval Academy. He spent a total of 12 years in the Navy, traveling Europe, the Orient and briefly served as personal escort to former President and Civil War General Grant. But his father needed him in the business, so Charles retired from the Navy and served as Chairman of the Board of International Harvester from 1902-1910. He was considered a natural leader, and used diplomacy and his knowledge of the world to build relationships for his family's company.

In addition to his business acumen, Charles studied art and attained proficiency as a portrait painter, encouraged by his lifelong friend and artist John Singer Sargent, whom he had met while in Spain. An avid art collector, Deering filled two of his castles in Spain with an extraordinary collection of artwork (most of which are now housed in the Art Institute of Chicago) including Rembrandts, Goyas and El Grecos.

Deering's other great passion, botany, sparked his interest in rural South Dade County. In 1913, he purchased the original 320 acres (which eventually would become 444 acres) of his estate located on Biscayne Bay in one of the early pioneer townships, the Town of Cutler.

Already on the property was the Richmond House; an 1896 two-story wood-frame building that had been the home of the pioneer Richmond family.

In 1900 the Richmond family opened "Richmond Cottage" as the first inn between Coconut Grove and Key West. In 1916 Deering remodeled the cottage and turned it into his private family winter home. A beautiful keyhole-shaped boat basin followed in 1918.

Then in 1922, Deering constructed a new residence called the Stone House, a 14,000-square-foot Mediterranean Revival-style mansion that also housed his growing art collection. In total he amassed more than 4,000 pieces and had one of the largest art collections in the world, which was appraised at $60 million dollars in 1922. The house was built with finely crafted details, bronze and copper-clad doors and windows, and 18-inch thick poured concrete walls to make the structure extremely resistant to fires and storms. He also laid a galvanized pipeline for fire suppression across the entire estate. Concern about safety extended to the room he built in the basement to hold his extensive wine collection. Steel doors and a swing-away bookcase guarded the wine and spirits in his Prohibition-era wine cellar.

The grounds have what is thought to be the largest virgin coastal tropical hardwood hammock in the continental U.S. The Deering Estate is a unique natural environment unlike any other in Dade County with an incredible array of plant life, including orchids, bromeliads and over 40 species of trees. The property has over 115 acres of the hammocks and 150 acres of pine rockland forests, one of the largest of this endangered environment.

The property is now a Miami-Dade County park where you can not only get a sense of how the families lived in the two homes, but of the love Deering had for the natural beauty of the area.

— Kendra Brennan and
Kathleen Kauffman

Vizcaya is an Italian Renaissance-style villa with formal gardens, built in 1916.

James Deering

James Deering is a Miami pioneer who got involved in an architectural project of far greater proportions than he had first contemplated when he decided to build a home in Coconut Grove. Deering was born in 1859, the son of William Deering, who established the Deering Harvester Company. By producing farming equipment that greatly facilitated the growth of commercial agriculture in the United States, the Deerings became one of America's wealthiest families.

Deering Harvester merged with its competitors in 1902 to become International Harvester, and James Deering served as vice president of the firm. Deering's father purchased land and built a home in Coconut Grove, and in 1910 James Deering decided to do the same. Deering already owned homes in Chicago, New York City, and outside of Paris, but in Miami—then a small city—he would create the most ambitious of his residences based on a variety of Italian and Spanish precedents, and called it Vizcaya.

Vizcaya was more than a home. Deering envisioned that the property would be self-sufficient and a village unto itself. A complex of buildings was constructed that contained staff quarters, maintenance, garages, barns, a stable, boathouses, dairy, poultry, and greenhouses. There was also a working farm with pastures and a citrus grove.

Deering traveled the world with his designer Paul Chalfin to assemble a collection of art, architectural elements and artifacts that included ancient Roman sculpture, Renaissance tapestries, Chinese ceramics, paintings and ornate furniture. Their purchases, along with pieces that were created especially for Vizcaya, were destined to reside inside the main house's 34 decorated rooms. Of the nearly completed Vizcaya in the midst of the Florida landscape, Paul Chalfin wrote, "It is almost as imposing as the Palazzo Pitti...if you can imagine the Palazzo Pitti standing on a lagoon in Africa."

Deering combined his interest in the art and history of Europe with his passion for the subtropical environment of Miami. He insisted on preserving the native vegetation and purposefully designed the house to take advantage of natural breezes. The formal gardens and the village, which was across the street from the main house, rendered Vizcaya the most complex and sophisticated private residence created in Florida to date.

Deering wintered at Vizcaya from 1916 to 1925. In his younger years he had been an active partygoer, boater, traveler and cultural ambassador; but by the time his house was finished, Deering's health was failing. Deering was generally described in his later years as a reticent man with impeccably proper manners leavened by a sense of humor. We know that his guests included inventor Thomas Alva Edison, painter John Singer Sargent (who was a friend of his half-brother Charles) and film star Lillian Gish. But one thing is for certain; there is no doubt that the man who created this extraordinary National Historic Landmark out of a mangrove swamp was truly visionary.

— Dr. Joel Hoffman, Executive Director
Vizcaya Museum and Gardens

From 1978 through 1981, the Villagers advocated for the preservation of the "Alamo" and assisted in its restoration.

Raymond Dillon

He was the handsome young Chief of Police (from 1915-1921). She was the young lady lots of old-timers remembered as "the prettiest girl in town." Ray and Adelaide Dillon had both come to Miami as teenagers with their families in the 1890s and soon after their marriage, built a house in Miami's first subdivision, Highland Park, in an area just south of Jackson Memorial Hospital.

The Dillons had many ties to the hospital, as all four Dillon children were born at home and were delivered by Dr. James Jackson himself. Daughter Elizabeth Dillon would eventually enter the Jackson Memorial School of Nursing in 1927, fulfilling a lifetime dream of becoming a nurse. One of her greatest joys as a child was to watch the construction of the City Hospital ("The Alamo" which opened in 1918.) A son-in-law, Dr. Ralph Allen, was on staff during his Miami medical career that began in the 1930's.

Ray and Adelaide Dillon were both avid gardeners. But it was Chief Dillon who made the big splash with plants. Their big 2-story bungalow-style house had a yard that covered a full half block in Highland Park because Ray knew he wanted to plant avocados, mangos, limes and a huge vegetable garden. And in fact, after several years there, he began his own botanical experiments.

The one everybody remembers is about hybridizing. He had read all about the science of creating new plants, and saw no reason why he couldn't combine two of his favorite things: cantaloupe and Cuban rum. He recruited his one-armed Bahamian gardener, a man named Lee, to help with the work. While Lee prepared the special garden spot, Ray walked over to the hospital and talked someone out of several racks for plasma bottles, a few feet of surgical tubing, and some hypodermic needles. Once the cantaloupe vines were growing, and had begun to set small melons, a plasma rack appeared beside each vine with a full rum bottle hanging upside down and surgical tubing running to a needle which was firmly planted into the forming melon.

Of course the neighbors became curious. As the melons grew, and the levels of rum went down, everyone became aware of the experiment and looked forward to the result.

Lee tended the plot regularly, kept it watered and replaced any rum bottle that became empty. After a few weeks, the whole neighborhood was assembled for the grand tasting. Chief Dillon sat at the kitchen table with the ripened melons and a big knife, as all the neighbors gathered around. With great drama, he cut the first melon, and sliced a piece to taste. He could not discern rum. So he tried another piece from the other side of the melon and handed out pieces to the wide-eyed neighbors. No one could say they tasted rum.

Suddenly with a knowing smile, the chief called Lee who was hanging around in the background, and asked him if he had any idea where all the rum had gone. Lee slowly and sheepishly admitted that each day when he tended the patch, he had sucked on each of the needles to be sure all were working well. As it became clear that the rum had all gone into Lee and not into the cantaloupes, the whole neighborhood had a good laugh. Chief Dillon wasn't upset, but instead turned it all into a party, and brought out a bottle of rum he had in the house and offered it all around.

— Ray Allen, grandson of Raymond Dillon

Marjory Stoneman Douglas lived in this 1924 house for more than 70 years.

Marjory Stoneman Douglas

During a lifetime that spanned 108 years, Marjory Stoneman Douglas (1890-1998) became the voice of the Everglades and a leading Florida environmentalist. Her many books and articles were written from a small cottage she built on Stewart Avenue in Coconut Grove, which she lived in for over 70 years with no stove, dishwasher or air-conditioning.

From the beginning, Marjory did not fit the mold for women of her time. After growing up in Taunton, Massachusetts, she attended Wellesley College then married a newspaper man 30 years her senior. Her father, whom she had not seen since she was 6 years old, was also in the newspaper field, as editor of the paper that would become the Miami Herald. Upon filing for her divorce, Marjory came to Miami in 1915 to work for her father.

She was an activist from a very early age, and her experiences would prepare her for a lifetime of community involvement. In 1916 she traveled with Mary Baird Bryan, William Jennings Bryan's wife, and two other women to Tallahassee to speak in support of women's right to vote, an experience about which she wrote: "All four of us spoke to a joint committee wearing our best hats. Talking to them was like talking to graven images. They never paid attention to us at all."

That same year, she joined the Navy, and after finding out she didn't like it, she requested a discharge and went to work for the Red Cross, where she was stationed in France. She came back to work for the newspaper, then in 1923 she finally set out on her own as a freelance writer.

Marjory loved to write fiction. From 1920 to 1990, she published 109 fiction articles and stories. However, her most notable work was *The Everglades: River of Grass*, which was published in 1947 after five years of research and sold out of its first printing a month after being released. The first line of the book, "There are no other Everglades in the world," has been called the most famous passage ever written about the Everglades.

Fame came to her not only for her extensive knowledge of the state and its vast wetland but for her talent as a dramatist. Although she only stood at 5-feet 2-inches and weighed 100 pounds, she was a great storyteller and could hold an audience in her grip. One of her many public appearances was before the Florida Cabinet in the late 1960s. It was convened by Governor Claude Kirk to hear a request that the state buy a former bombing range in the Everglades called the Holey Land. Among the speakers was this small elderly woman in her signature straw hat, pearls, flowered dress and sandals. She spoke way beyond her allotted time but nobody tried to stop her. When she finished, the Cabinet and the audience rose to give her a standing ovation. The Holey Land was bought.

In 1993, President Clinton awarded her the Presidential Medal of Freedom. Her legacy lives on, in the many schools, parks and buildings named after her, including the nature center on Key Biscayne and the State's natural resources building in Tallahassee. But most importantly, her beloved River of Grass lives on because of her dedication and attention.

— Juanita Greene, Conservation Chair
Friends of the Everglades

Dr. Eleanor Galt Simmons, the first woman to practice medicine in the Miami area, built this barn in 1892 out of native limestone and Dade County pine to house her horse and carriage. The oldest surviving structure in the county still in its original location, it later housed the study of Dr. David Fairchild.

Dr. David Fairchild

Dr. David Fairchild was one of the most influential horticulturalists and plant collectors in the United States. Fairchild served as Head of the Office of Foreign Seed and Plant Introduction for the Department of Agriculture, and during that time (1897-1928) he would introduce over 30,000 varieties of plants into the United States.

David Fairchild had already traveled the tropics of the Old World extensively before he ever set foot in Florida in 1898. What struck Fairchild most was not the remoteness of the Miami area or the difficulties he would encounter, but that here was a zone in which some of the tropical fruits and flowering trees he had encountered in Java and elsewhere could actually be grown.

David Fairchild did not make a permanent move to Miami until 1928, when he and wife Marian built their home and an introductory garden for his plants at the Kampong (a Malay word for a collection or cluster of buildings for an extended family). He and Marian would entertain prominent citizens such as Henry Ford, Thomas Edison, Henry Firestone and Marian's own father, Alexander Graham Bell.

David and Marian Fairchild utilized both The Kampong and the adjoining property Hissar (owned by Marian's sister, Elsie Grosvenor), to grow mangos from seeds gathered from around the world by themselves and the "Plant Explorers," a group funded by the Department of Plant Introduction, then under the directorship of David Fairchild.

Several varieties of mangos proved too acidic, stringy or otherwise unsuitable for most palates even when ripe. David and Marian knew these were used in their native countries primarily for the making of condiments, so they decided to consume them in the same way, discovering in the process which mangos produced the best chutneys.

The family always had Sunday night supper together at The Kampong and it became a great family occasion, with three generations (plus assorted friends) tasting and grading the most recent batch of chutney.

My mother, Barbara Fairchild Muller, continued to make small batches of chutney in the summer and fall, choosing various green mangos from both The Kampong and Hissar properties (see page 88). These she handed out for family use and as Christmas gifts to friends. Her preserves soon became so popular that Mother and two other University of Miami faculty wives, Barbara Bitter and Faith Jackson, decided to produce the chutney commercially under the trademark Kampong, Inc. in the back kitchen of The Kampong. All three partners and their kids got involved in some capacity, from picking, peeling, and slicing mangos, to stirring great vats of boiling and fragrant "glop," to bottling, labeling, and packing gold gift boxes with a red "Garuda Bird" printed on the top.

When Marian Fairchild died, and the Sweeney family acquired The Kampong, they bought out Kampong Inc. and the task of making "Kampong Chutney" fell to the capable care of Bernice Russell.

I still use my mother's small batch original recipe, which when commercialized into 50-gallon batches had to be adjusted to retain the flavor and texture of the original product. We used to compare different "vintages" of chutney at a yearly "Rijstaffel," (see recipe page 153) a festive treat for kids and adults alike and a way to travel the world through tastes.

— Hélène Muller Pancoast, Granddaughter
and Kit Pancoast Nagamura,
Great-Granddaughter of Dr. David Fairchild

Built in 1924, the Van Dyke building was where Fisher would showcase the city from his office on the top floor.

Carl Graham Fisher

Though not one of South Florida's earliest pioneers, Carl Fisher (1874-1939) was the one who transformed the mangrove swamp east of Miami into a fashionable winter resort, launched a promotional campaign up north, and first put Miami Beach on the map. His own personal story was no less remarkable a transformation. From rags-to-riches origins in Indianapolis, he made a multimillion-dollar fortune in automobile headlights by the age of 38, built the Indianapolis Speedway in 1909 and initiated its famous 500-mile race two years later, then organized the construction of the nation's first interstate paved roads: the Lincoln and Dixie Highways.

In the meantime, Fisher and his child-bride Jane had bought a winter home in Miami in 1910, but a life of leisure didn't suit his restless energy. He spent the next 25 years and nearly all his fortune on the development of Miami Beach. Down the center of his first tract of land he laid out Lincoln Road, which became the social center of the infant city. (Fisher named nothing for himself, but instead honored his hero, Abraham Lincoln – unusual this far south!) Here he built the Lincoln Hotel, a community theater, an indoor tennis court, a Congregational church, and, in 1924, the seven-story Lincoln Building. It was the tallest building in town at the time. It housed the offices of Fisher's many

real estate companies, and the entire top floor, with a private elevator, was Mr. Fisher's own office. From the balcony he could survey his domain and point out the most desirable lots to prospective buyers. The building was sold and renamed the Van Dyke in 1938.

The Fishers built their own oceanfront mansion at the east end of Lincoln Road in 1914. In her memoir, Jane described those early days: "With no hotels or stores on the Beach, our home was headquarters for all who visited or pioneered. I might have been keeping house on a desert island. Every item of food, every stick of furniture or building material, even the water we drank, was transported by wagon or barge or truck across Biscayne Bay. Canned stuff was ordered by the crate from the mail-order houses. Among my domestic duties was the daily warfare against the insects, land crabs and snakes that retreated toward the (house) in advance of the dredges filling in their marsh retreats."

— *Carolyn Klepser*

Dr. Jackson's office is now the headquarters for Dade Heritage Trust, a non-profit historic preservation organization.

Dr. James M. Jackson

The Miami of 1896 was a frontier town, where the living wasn't easy. The downtown was comprised of wooden buildings that looked more like a stop along the Santa Fe Trail (with livery stables and blacksmith shops) rather than a city set amongst the tropical splendor of the aquamarine sea, the clear blue sky, and the emerald richness of an exotic landscape unlike any other place in the nation. Dirt roadways churned into muck by the passing of so many horses, the infernal mosquitoes that could drive men mad and the onerous heat that sapped the strength of even the most fit tested the mettle of those courageous early pioneers.

In these primitive conditions, yellow fever, typhoid, smallpox and consumption ravaged the population at a time when there was little in the way of medical care. One of the few who rose to the task was Dr. James M. Jackson, originally from Bronson, Florida. Dr. Jackson graduated from the Bellevue (New York) Medical College and came to Miami in 1896 as the physician-surgeon for Henry Flagler's Florida East Coast (F.E.C.) Railway.

With the lack of medical supplies and few medical doctors to perform surgical procedures, many a Miamian fell victim to maladies that otherwise would not have been life threatening. There were no anesthesiologists, so chloroform had to do. One story is told of an operation performed in a horse stable, where one person had the task of shooing the flies away with a palm frond.

Dr. Jackson built an office and a small surgery in 1905 to accommodate the young city's growing need. That same year, Flagler built the Florida East Coast Railway Extension Hospital for the F.E.C. workers. While the railroad workers were cared for, the disenfranchised (including the poor and African-Americans) had nowhere to go. In 1908 a group calling themselves "The Friendly Society" began their efforts to build a private hospital— an 18-bed facility completed in 1909 and called it the "Miami Hospital." Ultimately the City of Miami took over the hospital operations, and in 1916 constructed the first building that became the nucleus for the massive complex we know today as Jackson Memorial Hospital.

Around 1917, Dr. Jackson's home and office were moved from their original location and barged down the bay a short distance to the present location (190 SE 12th Terrace). Fittingly, today the County's largest not-for-profit historic preservation organization, Dade Heritage Trust, occupies the office and surgery.

Dr. Jackson was a leader in almost every aspect of Miami's early history. He was a founding member and later president of the Dade County Medical Association; he was the local agent for the State Board of Health and in 1914 organized the Miami City Board of Health. Dr. Jackson's legacy lives on not only in the hospital complex that bears his name but also in his heirs, most of whom continued his dedication to the medical profession.

— *Ellen J. Uguccioni*

The former home of Hugh M. Matheson in
Coconut Grove, designed in 1925 by Walter DeGarmo.

Hugh M. Matheson

Hugh Matheson (1886 - 1952) was the son of a prominent Miami pioneer and would go on to become an important part of Miami's early history. Hugh was the one actually responsible for convincing his father, William J., to buy property in Coconut Grove. Hugh and his younger brother, Malcolm, were attending what is now known as Ransom Everglades preparatory school in 1902. At the time, the school operated in the Adirondacks in the fall and spring, and Coconut Grove in the winter. He invited his father down to visit and sail on the bay. His father immediately fell in love with the area and returned a year later to buy 15 acres on the bay in Coconut Grove on which to build a winter home.

Over the next few years Hugh's father also bought property on Key Biscayne and built a large estate with a lagoon on the tip of Mashta point, where he would entertain lavishly. The estate included warehouses, barns, workers' dormitories, and docks for boats and barges. By 1908 Hugh's father had purchased the northern two thirds of the island, or about 1,700 acres. He began clearing the land and experimenting with limes, mangoes and avocados; however, the trees were too close to the salt spray to be commercially successful.

Hugh graduated from Yale and worked at one of his father's chemical companies where he would eventually become sick from lead poisoning. He was sent back to Coconut Grove to recover, and subsequently fell in love and married his nurse, Ligouri Hardy in 1911. As his father's ventures became more diversified, Hugh was needed to manage the family's properties and investments.

It was up to Hugh to see that the swamps were drained and filled, the roads cleared and that the yacht basins were built. He expanded his father's grove facilities, including new quarters for all of the construction workers, and planted coconut trees by the thousands. By 1915, more than eighteen miles of unpaved roadways were created where originally there had been none.

Hugh joined Biscayne Bay Yacht Club in 1912, the year his father became commodore. Hugh was an avid sailor and in 1937, when he himself was commodore, won Biscayne Bay Yacht Club's Golden Jubilee Race, a 30-mile triangular race off Miami Beach; finished second in the Miami-Nassau Race; then capped off a great racing season by winning the Saint Petersburg-Havana and Lipton Cup events, the modern day equivalent of winning the grand slam in tennis.

Hugh and his father William initiated a number of projects that would have a great impact on the community and residents' quality of life. In 1915, they were founding members of the Audubon Society of Coconut Grove along with Kirk Munroe and Charles Deering. In 1916, they were responsible for putting in the first telephone system. That same year, they also established the Coconut Grove Public Utilities Company on Devon Road, which would remain the Grove's only waterworks until 1925.

Hugh would go on to serve 2 terms as mayor of Coconut Grove from 1921-25, and during his term fought the annexation of Coconut Grove by the city of Miami. To this day, the Matheson family continues to be active in the advocacy for the environment and local community.

— Bruce C. Matheson,
grandson of Hugh M. Matheson

127

The Merrick House, located on Coral Way, was the boyhood home of Coral Gables founder George Merrick.

George Edgar Merrick

George Merrick was the oldest son of remarkable parents. His father, Solomon, was a Yale-educated minister and his mother, Althea, a college graduate artist. The Merrick family came to South Florida in 1899 when the City of Miami was only three years old. The move was prompted by the death of a child during a severe winter in Duxbury, Massachusetts where Solomon was the minister at the Pilgrim Congregational Church. Aided by Rev. James Bolton of the Coconut Grove Union Church, they purchased—sight unseen—a 160 acre homestead in the backcountry.

When 13-year-old George and his father arrived to prepare the homestead for the rest of the family's arrival, they found an isolated, wooden shack and a barn made of barrel staves. The rocky pineland had only a small clearing planted in guava trees. The contrast from their previous life was startling, to say the least.

George went to work in the fields with the black Bahamians from Coconut Grove. To survive, he sold the guavas in Coconut Grove and later vegetables, which were grown on today's Granada Golf Course. His father's dream was to plant grapefruit trees and turn the barren land into a profitable grapefruit grove. In 1901, to help make ends meet until the groves began to bear, Solomon Merrick became minister of the Coconut Grove Congregational Church— later Plymouth Congregational.

By 1907, the grapefruit groves had begun to bear just as Solomon Merrick promised and George was able to go to Rollins College—his first schooling since age 13. After two years at Rollins, he went to New York Law School for a year, until his father's deteriorating health caused him to return home to help manage the groves.

About the time George went to college, his mother designed a commodious new home for the family but due to financial problems, it was not completed until 1910. The family named the coral rock (oolithic limestone) home Coral Gables. It was the finest home in the backcountry.

After Solomon Merrick's death in 1911, George took over management of the groves and two years later entered the Miami real estate scene. He dreamed of creating a planned community on his family's now 1200 acre Coral Gables Plantation. But before he touched Coral Gables, he subdivided acreage and sold lots all over Miami to raise capital and learn the business.

In November 1921, with a plan in place, he sold the first lots in Coral Gables. With strict architectural guidelines, he created beautiful entrances and plazas, designed by his artist-uncle Denman Fink. He launched a national marketing campaign that helped create the real estate boom of the 1920s. He made millions but poured all his profits back into his dream city that was incorporated in April 1925.

Although the boom ended following the catastrophic 1926 hurricane, George continued to pour all his money into trying to save Coral Gables. By the summer of 1928, however, he had spent all his money and he lost control of the place he created.

One only needs to drive through Coral Gables to feel George Merrick's legacy. But to really understand the genesis and genius of his creative mind, a visit to the Coral Gables Merrick House is a must. Purchased by the City of Coral Gables in 1973, it remains a living monument to a remarkable family whose son transformed a wilderness into a "City Beautiful."

— Arva Moore Parks

The octagonal "stair hall" was the original dining room before the house was lifted and a new first floor inserted below. The open-air upper level served as the attic.

Ralph Middleton Munroe

The Barnacle Historic State Park, tucked away on busy Main Highway, is one of Miami's favorite historic places. It is not only the area's oldest home in its original location but a special window into what has been called "The Era of the Bay" –before there was a Miami.

Its builder, Ralph Munroe, fell in love with the South Florida wilderness in 1877. As a young sailing enthusiast, he was fascinated by what he described as a "mysterious, remote and legend haunted region—set in a scene of warm and brilliant sunlight on blue water lapping green islands and covering coral reefs." After a brief visit, he returned to his home in Staten Island, New York, married and became a father. In 1881, when his wife Eva became ill with tuberculosis, he remembered the warmth of South Florida's winter and brought his dying wife to the Miami area in an attempt to restore her health. While camping on the north bank of the Miami River, he met Charles and Isabella Peacock who had come from England six years earlier. Despite the devotion of the young husband and loving care of Isabella Peacock, Eva Munroe died and was buried in Miami. (Her body was later reinterred in Coconut Grove.)

When Munroe returned to New York, he learned that his infant daughter had also died. Cast adrift by a tragic and dramatic change of his life's direction, he longed to return to the place he buried his wife. Returning to South Florida during the winter of 1882, he brought his camera and took the earliest known photographs of South Florida. He also fell in love with the pristine beauty he documented.

Because the wilderness had no place to house visitors, he convinced Charles and Isabella Peacock to open an inn in today's Coconut Grove. In 1886, with the inn almost completed, Munroe arrived with a group of sophisticated northern tourists, many of whom later became permanent residents. That same year, he purchased 40 acres from Coconut Grove pioneer John Frow for $400 and his sharpie (a shallow draft sailboat) named Kingfish.

In 1887, Munroe built a boathouse on the bay and from there launched the Biscayne Bay Yacht Club—Miami's oldest private institution. Four years later, he designed his home that he called the Barnacle. It reflected his strong appreciation of the environment. Built high on the ridge, he designed it with a wide veranda and a clerestory window to capture the southeast breeze.

He also understood and valued Biscayne Bay. He created a new type of centerboard sailboat called the Presto-type, that was not only seaworthy but also at home in shallow bay waters. One of the area's first environmentalists, he tried to protect the bay from island builders and fought for the green turtle from being over-hunted. He protested when his neighbors would dump waste into the bay, introduced septic tanks and tried to convince fellow pioneers that sea walls actually accelerate erosion near the walls themselves.

After he remarried and his two children Wirth and Patty were born, Munroe enlarged the Barnacle by jacking up the home and building a new first floor underneath. After his death, his son Wirth and his wife Mary and their sons Bill and Charlie continued to live in the home. In 1973, the surviving family members sold the Barnacle to the State of Florida. This sale not only preserved the Barnacle but stopped inappropriate development from continuing down Main Highway. Today, everyone who visits the Barnacle is able to experience and learn from Ralph Munroe's world and appreciate his enduring legacy.

— Arva Moore Parks

131

Father and son builders Caleb and Harlan Trapp built the first stone house in Coconut Grove in 1889, which was later enlarged in 1929.

The Trapp Family

Caleb Trapp moved from Iowa in 1887 to Coconut Grove with his wife, Henrietta Rhodes Trapp and son Harlan. They settled on a tract of land fronting current-day South Bayshore Drive, and lived in a palmetto-thatched hut for over a year. Every time it rained, all their possessions would have to be dragged out of the hut to dry in the sun.

Caleb, who was 70 years of age, had been a brick mason, so he and son Harlan set out to build a stone house on the property. While the early pioneer homes were constructed of wood and had dirt floors, the Trapp Homestead featured masonry construction. Using chisels and hatchets, they quarried the native oolitic limestone from the cliff for the walls of their home. Some of the blocks were 18 inches thick. The beams were made from huge timbers that Harlan retrieved from the beach on the ocean that had drifted in from foundered timber ships.

Nine years later Harlan returned to Iowa to marry his childhood sweetheart, Minnie. When Minnie arrived on the shores of Biscayne Bay at the Trapp property, she had to trudge up a mud path 600 feet, through saw grass, intense mosquitoes and soldier crabs scuttling out from underneath her feet. As she was wondering how she would ever endure this unfortunate place now called home, she arrived at the house and turned to look at the bay. Gazing at the reflection of the setting sun on the water, casting gold and purple colors across the bay, Minnie Trapp figured that living in a place such as this would bring great joy.

The Trapp families were significant members of the Coconut Grove community. Henrietta Trapp started and served as the first teacher for Coconut Grove's first public school. She hosted the first Dade County teachers' examination in her stone house. Son Harlan was also a teacher, and was one of the founding members of Biscayne Bay Yacht Club. The Trapps' daughter Emma also taught at the same Coconut Grove School. Mrs. Trapp's brother, Harlan Rhodes, was an early landowner in Coconut Grove and a member of the Dade County School Board. Mr. Rhodes owned a significant amount of land in Coconut Grove, and modern-day South Bayshore was actually named Rhodes Boulevard in the 1890s.

Early existence in South Florida was not easy for the Trapps, but they succeeded. Initially, they could only reach Miami by boat because bears and panthers inhabited the woods between Coconut Grove and Miami. They would often use their homestead to welcome visitors when the nearby Peacock Inn was full, and Henrietta always left a light in an upper window to serve as a beacon for mariners who had lost their way.

The Trapps became involved with making Coontie starch (Coontie is a plant the Seminole Indians called "arrow root") and cultivated avocados, which they sold to the local hotels. One avocado they cultivated, the Trapp avocado, was famous in agricultural communities. Today, Trapp Avenue continues to run through a part of Coconut Grove as a reminder of this true pioneering family.

— *Victor Mendelson*

SUPPER IS SERVED

Meats, Poultry and Quiche

"At the Montgomery Botanical Center, former home of Robert Montgomery, founder of Fairchild Tropical Garden, Villager grants funded the installation of air-conditioning systems in the main house and restoration of the guest house."

THE VILLAGERS

TENDERLOIN

with Green Peppercorn Sauce

Ingredients

**2 8-ounce steak fillets,
cut 1½ inches thick**

1 tablespoon butter

3 tablespoons brandy

½ cup heavy cream

**2 teaspoons
green peppercorns in brine,
drained, coarsely chopped**

**2 teaspoons
Grey Poupon mustard**

Directions

Generously sprinkle the fillets with fresh cracked pepper. Melt butter in sauté pan, and cook steaks until desired tenderness, approximately 4 minutes per side for medium-rare. Remove and rest the meat, covered with foil, while making sauce.

Place the brandy in the same pan, ignite, and bring to a boil, scraping up any pan drippings. Add peppercorns, mustard, and cream. Cook until sauce thickens, stirring constantly.

Place a small amount of the sauce on the dinner plate, place a fillet on top, then spoon more sauce over the fillets.

Serves 2

Detail of front door of the Montgomery Home

STEAK

À La Stroganoff

Ingredients

2 pounds round steak

½ cup flour

1 teaspoon salt

1 teaspoon paprika

¼ cup olive oil

½ cup chopped onion

1 10.5-ounce can
beef consommé

½ cup water

1 bay leaf

½ teaspoon thyme

½ teaspoon oregano

1 4-ounce can mushroom caps

2 tablespoons sherry, optional

1 cup sour cream

Directions

Remove gristle and fat from meat, and cut into small bite size pieces. Shake in a sack with the flour (seasoned with the salt and paprika), and brown in hot oil.

Add onion and sauté until just tender. Add consommé, water and herbs. Cover and simmer for 45 minutes to 1 hour or until meat is tender, adding more water if necessary. If gravy isn't thick, mix in a little cornstarch (pre-mixed with cold water) to gravy.

Before serving, stir in the mushrooms, sherry and sour cream. Heat and serve over hot rice or egg noodles.

Serves 4 to 6

CORNED BEEF

and Cabbage

Ingredients

2 to 4 pounds corned beef brisket

7 sweet onions, sliced

2 large bags baby carrots

1 bag small whole potatoes, red or new golden

2 heads cabbage, quartered, core intact on each piece

1 cinnamon stick

12 whole allspice

6 garlic peppercorns, whole

12 mélange peppercorns, whole

4 bay leaves

12 whole cloves

½ teaspoon dried dill, or dill seed

4 tablespoons brown sugar

1 bottle Killian Red Ale

Directions

Arrange all the dry ingredients in a large iron pot, turkey roaster, or any pot large enough to handle everything sort of in a single layer. Pour the ale over, and add water to barely cover all. Cook over LOWEST setting on top of stove for 8-9 hours.

Let meat rest for at least 15 minutes. Set aside 3 cups of the cooking liquid for the White Sauce (to go with the potatoes). Take out all ingredients and arrange on a platter while meat is cooling. Slice meat thinly and add to the platter. Serve with several mustards (spicy, mild yellow, brown, champagne or maple syrup mustard).

Serves 6

White Sauce (for the potatoes)

3 cups cooking liquid

1 tablespoon garlic salt

4 ounces heavy whipping cream

2 tablespoons potato starch

1 tablespoon dill

Directions

Stir the garlic salt, cream, and potato starch into the cooking liquid. Cook on low heat until the sauce thickens. Add dill, stir, and pour into a gravy boat.

HAWAIIAN PORK PATTIES

with Pineapple–Papaya Sauce

Ingredients

1 pound ground pork

3 tablespoons breadcrumbs

2 tablespoons grated
yellow onion

¼ teaspoon cayenne pepper

1 tablespoon light brown sugar

1 teaspoon olive oil

¼ teaspoon salt

⅛ teaspoon black pepper

4 Kaiser rolls

Directions

Mix the ingredients for the sauce together.
Mix the pork, breadcrumbs, onion, cayenne, sugar
and ⅓ cup of the sauce until evenly combined.
Shape into four 1-inch thick patties. Brush the
burgers with oil, then season with salt and pepper.

Grill over medium heat, turning once, about 6
minutes a side. Baste with some of the sauce and
grill for 2 more minutes. To serve, place burgers on
rolls and spoon on remaining Pineapple-Papaya
sauce. Top with lettuce, tomato, thinly sliced
pineapple, or onion slices to your taste.

Serves 4

Pineapple - Papaya Sauce

4 tablespoons crushed
pineapple, thoroughly drained

3 tablespoons fresh papaya,
finely diced

⅔ cup basic barbecue sauce

1 tablespoon soy sauce

Directions

Mix all the ingredients together, cover and
refrigerate until needed.

FAJITAS

Ingredients

⅛ cup oil

⅛ cup sesame oil

¼ cup soy sauce

3 tablespoons red wine vinegar

2 tablespoons brown sugar

¼ teaspoon grated
fresh ginger root

2 large garlic cloves, minced

½ teaspoon red pepper flakes

2 teaspoons sesame seeds

2 tablespoons limejuice

4 chopped green onions

2 pounds flank or skirt steak

1 teaspoon sesame oil

3 green peppers, chopped

3 medium onions,
cut in thin rings

3 tomatoes, seeded, chopped

1 cup each, guacamole, salsa,
and sour cream

8 to 12 flour tortillas

Directions

Combine the first 11 ingredients and marinate the steak overnight, or at least 2 hours. Grill 5 to 10 minutes on each side; keep warm and slice when ready to serve.

Preheat oven to 250 degrees. Fry the green peppers, onions, and tomatoes in 1 teaspoon sesame oil, until slightly soft. Keep warm until ready to serve.

Warm tortillas in the oven, wrapped in a dish towel to keep moist. Put the guacamole, salsa, and sour cream in individual bowls. Serve the tortillas with all the fixings.

Serves 4 to 6

MINCED BEEF MIX

This was a favorite of my kids when they were young.

Ingredients

½ cup onion, chopped

1 tablespoon butter

2 pounds ground beef

⅔ cup catsup

½ cup water

¼ cup celery, chopped

2 tablespoons lemon juice

1 tablespoon brown sugar

1½ teaspoons Worcestershire

1½ teaspoons salt

1 teaspoon vinegar

¼ teaspoon dry mustard

Directions

Saute onion in butter, add beef, and brown lightly. Drain off excess fat. Add rest of the ingredients. Simmer, covered, for 30 minutes.

Serves 4 to 6

Variations

• It's a great sloppy joe recipe. Just scoop the mix onto your favorite hamburger bun.

• Just use the bottom half of a hamburger bun, the mix, and broil a slice of cheese on top.

• You can transform it into chili by using ⅓ cup of the mix, 1 15-ounce can kidney beans, including liquid, ½ to 1-cup tomato juice, and 2 to 3 teaspoons chili powder.

ORIENTAL MEATLOAF

Ingredients

1½ pounds ground beef

½ cup breadcrumbs

2 eggs beaten

½ cup chopped onions

½ cup red bell pepper, chopped

1 small can water chestnuts, chopped

3 tablespoons ketchup

2 tablespoons soy sauce

Topping

1 tablespoon brown sugar

2 tablespoons ketchup

1 tablespoon soy sauce

½ teaspoon dry mustard

Directions

Preheat oven to 350 degrees. Combine the beef, breadcrumbs, eggs, onions, bell pepper, water chestnuts, 3 tablespoons ketchup, and soy sauce. Make into a loaf.

Make the topping with the brown sugar, ketchup, soy sauce, and dry mustard. Spread the topping over the loaf and bake for 1 hour.

Serves 4

TUSCAN BEEF & CANNELLINI STEW

Ingredients

2 pounds boneless stew beef,
cut into bite size pieces

¼ cup flour

3 cups beef broth (or a 10-ounce
can beef broth mixed with 1 can
tomato soup, 1 can water)

1 cup dry red wine

1 14-ounce can diced
Italian-style tomatoes

1 medium onion, chopped

2 celery ribs, chopped

3 large carrots
cut in 1-inch pieces

2 bay leaves

2 garlic cloves,
crushed and minced

2 15-ounce cans
cannellini beans, drained

1 teaspoon basil

Sliced mushrooms, pearl onions
and spinach, optional

Directions

Toss the beef with the flour and brown well in
a Dutch oven. Add the rest of the ingredients
except beans, basil and optional ingredients.
Bring to a boil and then reduce to simmer, cook
for 2 hours (or put in a preheated oven at
350 degrees for 2 hours).

Then, mash ¼ of the beans, add to the stew with
the remaining beans, and optional ingredients, if
using. Continue to cook for 30 minutes.

Serves 8

SZECHWAN CHICKEN

The Pruitt Family's all time favorite recipe. Delicious!

Ingredients

1 tablespoon vegetable oil, or more

2 whole chicken breasts

3 tablespoons cornstarch

3 garlic cloves, minced

5 tablespoons soy sauce

½ tablespoon white wine vinegar

1 teaspoon sugar

¼ cup water

2 green onions, sliced thin

⅛ to ¼ teaspoon cayenne pepper

Directions

Split the chicken breast in half. Cut chicken into ½-inch cubes. Toss chicken cubes in cornstarch. Heat oil in large non-stick skillet. Add chicken and garlic. Lightly brown chicken. Add soy sauce, vinegar, sugar, and water to skillet. Cover. Cook 3 minutes or until chicken is cooked. Uncover. Add green onions and cayenne. Heat 2 minutes longer. Serve with rice.

Serves 4

SHOPPERS CHICKEN

After a day out of the house shopping, this is quick and easy, not to mention delicious! If you double the sauce you will have a generous amount to spoon over the rice.

Ingredients

3 whole chicken breasts cut into quarters

1 cup light sour cream

2 tablespoons lemon juice

1 teaspoon salt

1 teaspoon paprika

½ cup melted butter, optional

White rice for 6

Directions

Preheat oven to 350 degrees. Combine sour cream, lemon juice, salt and paprika. Place the chicken in a buttered baking dish. Spread sour cream mix on top. Pour the melted butter over the top. Bake for 40 minutes uncovered.

Serves 6

ARTICHOKE CHICKEN CASSEROLE

Double the recipe and you have a great dinner party dish. Serve with rice or noodles, whole green beans, a salad and dessert, and wait for the compliments.

Ingredients

3 whole chicken breasts

2 cans of cream of chicken soup mixed with 1 cup water

2 14-ounce cans quartered artichoke hearts

1 cup low fat mayonnaise

1 teaspoon lemon juice

1 teaspoon curry powder, or to taste

2 tablespoons melted butter

1½ cups extra sharp cheddar or mozzarella

¾ to 1¼ cup bread crumbs

Directions

Pre-cook the chicken in a little of the chicken soup mix. Preheat oven to 350 degrees.

Grease a 9 x 13 x 2-inch baking dish. Drain the artichokes and arrange in the dish. Spread chicken on top. Combine the rest of the soup mixture with the mayonnaise, lemon juice and curry powder. Pour over chicken. Top with cheese, and sprinkle breadcrumbs on top. Bake for 25 minutes.

Serves 6

AUNTIE JANIE'S AFRICAN CHICKEN

This is a classic featured for the last 16 years at the Annual Family 4th of July gathering at Jane & Kalle Petrick's home in Woodstock, NY. Tastes marvelous when made a day ahead, and makes an excellent buffet meal for large groups.

Ingredients

3 pounds boneless chicken breasts or thighs

2 cups peanut butter

2 cups Louisiana style hot sauce (Must be Louisiana style, not Tabasco or other hot sauce. This gives the dish its special flavor and will not make the food taste "hot" once it is cooked.)

6 cups chicken stock

Peanut oil, enough to cover the bottom of heavy stew pot

Directions

Heat peanut oil in heavy stew pot. Brown the chicken in oil, on both sides.

In a large bowl, mix the peanut butter and the hot sauce into a paste. Slowly add stock to the paste to make a sauce. Remove chicken from heat and stir in sauce with chicken, its drippings and oil.

Stir to coat and blend completely. Return to cook over low medium heat. Stir frequently from the bottom, being sure sauce does not stick. Add more chicken stock if you need to thin the sauce.

Cook until chicken is falling apart tender. Serve over rice with Auntie Janie's collard greens, page 186.

Serves 6 to 8

BAKED CHICKEN

with Guava Sauce

*A recipe inspired by Althea Merrick, mother of
Coral Gables founder George Merrick.*

Ingredients

1 scallion chopped

½ small onion chopped

2 cloves garlic chopped

1 tablespoon olive oil

6 skinless/boneless
chicken breast halves

1 large guava sliced,
to serve on the side

Directions

Preheat oven to 350 degrees. Mix the first three
ingredients with the olive oil.

Season the chicken with the flavored olive oil.
Add salt/pepper to taste. Marinate for 20 minutes.
Bake the chicken on a greased baking sheet for
25 minutes.

Spoon the prepared Guava Sauce over the chicken
and bake 10 minutes more. Serve with sliced guava
on the side.

Serves 6

Guava Sauce

1 cup guava pulp chopped

½ cup tomato sauce

¼ whole fresh ginger diced

1 tablespoon brown sugar

1 cup guava juice

4 cups water

¼ cup white cane vinegar

Directions

Combine all of the ingredients and
boil for 15 minutes.

INDIAN CHICKEN

This is a fun buffet dish. Serve with basmati rice.

Ingredients

1 whole chicken, or boned and skinned legs and thighs

1 large onion, minced

6 to 8 whole cloves

Peppercorns, to taste

1 inch piece fresh ginger, peeled and sliced

1 clove of garlic, minced

2 teaspoons curry powder

1 teaspoon garam masala (can be found in Indian or middle eastern groceries)

1 large jalapeno pepper, remove seeds and mince

1 15-ounce can whole tomatoes

1 small container plain yogurt

Directions

Cut chicken into pieces or use already boned and skinned legs and thighs. In a large frying pan, sauté the minced onion in melted Crisco along with the whole cloves and peppercorns. Add the ginger and the minced garlic clove.

Add the curry powder, garam masala, and the jalapeno pepper and sauté these spices. Add one can whole tomatoes to the chicken and cook about an hour and a half at a low heat until tender. Before serving add a small container of plain yogurt. Serve after the yogurt is heated.

Serves 8

PARTY CHICKEN

Ingredients

8 chicken breasts, split, boned and skin removed

8 slices bacon

4 ounces chipped beef

½ pint sour cream

1 can cream of mushroom soup

½ cup white wine

Directions

Preheat oven to 275 degrees. Wash and flatten the chicken. Wrap a chicken breast (that's been divided) around chipped beef, and then wrap chicken with bacon. This should end up about the size of your fist. Place in a 9 x 13 x 2-inch baking dish. Mix the sour cream, soup and wine to taste and pour over chicken. Bake for 3 hours uncovered.

Serves 8

CHICKEN

with Saffron, Green Olives & Mint

*With their juicy flesh, thighs can be reheated several times and never dry out.
This is a favorite part of the chicken for many chefs and foodies.
Serve on a bed of couscous.*

Ingredients

**12 chicken thighs,
2½ - 3 pounds total,
can be skinless and boneless**

Salt and pepper

All-purpose flour, for dredging

¼ cup extra-virgin olive oil

2 large red onions, thinly sliced

½ teaspoon saffron threads

1 cup small green olives

1 medium carrot, finely chopped

3 cups chicken stock

½ cup fresh mint leaves

Directions

Season the chicken thighs liberally with salt and pepper and dredge in flour. In a Dutch oven, heat the olive oil until smoking. Add 6 thighs at a time and brown well on all sides over medium-high heat. Transfer to a plate and repeat with the remaining thighs. When well browned, remove the thighs and add the sliced onions and saffron to the Dutch oven. Cook over low heat until the onions have softened, 8 to 10 minutes. Add the olives, carrot, and stock and bring to a boil.

Return the chicken pieces to the Dutch oven, submerging them in the stock and bring to a boil. Lower the heat to a simmer, cover the pot tightly and simmer 1 hour. Remove the lid and cook 10 minutes uncovered.

Remove the chicken thighs from the Dutch oven and arrange on a platter. Season the sauce with salt and pepper and stir in the mint leaves. Pour the sauce over the chicken thighs and serve on a bed of couscous.

Serves 6

PARMESAN CRUSTED CHICKEN

Children love the Parmesan crust and the sweet and tangy sauce.
Serve with sautéed spinach and oven fried or mashed potatoes.
Your guests will think you cooked all day!

Ingredients

½ cup extra virgin olive oil

½ cup good quality
grated Parmesan cheese

4 tablespoons minced
fresh marjoram

4 garlic cloves, minced

3 pounds of assorted pieces
of chicken with bone in
(if using breasts cut in ½)

Salt and fresh ground
pepper to taste

Directions

Preheat the oven to 400 degrees. Make a paste of the first 4 ingredients. In a large bowl, toss with the chicken pieces. Arrange the chicken pieces, skin side up, on a large rimmed baking sheet and season with salt and pepper.

Bake for about 35-45 minutes, or until lightly browned and just cooked through.

Serves 6

Balsamic Vinegar Butter Sauce

1 cup Imagine brand
No-Chicken Broth

½ cup balsamic vinegar

2 tablespoons unsalted butter

Directions

While the chicken is cooking combine the broth and vinegar and boil over high heat until reduced to ⅔ cup, about 10-20 minutes. Remove from the heat and whisk in the butter, 1 tablespoon at a time, until smooth. Transfer the chicken to plates, spoon some of the sauce on top and serve. Serve the rest of the sauce in a gravy boat.

BROCCOLI CHEESE QUICHE

This delicious crust-less broccoli quiche soufflé is from the August Seven Inn, in Daytona Beach, a historic Bed & Breakfast, which was founded in 1889 and was the guesthouse of James Gamble of Proctor & Gamble.

Ingredients

2 cups broccoli florets

2 tablespoons olive oil

1 tablespoon butter

1 small white onion, minced

18 eggs

1 tablespoon oregano

1 tablespoon basil

2 cloves garlic, minced

¼ teaspoon dill

3 cups light cream

1 teaspoon celery salt

2 cups shredded Italian cheese

Directions

Preheat oven to 350 degrees. Grease 8 10-ounce ramekins with cooking spray.

Sauté the broccoli in the olive oil and butter on low heat for approximately 2 minutes, stirring constantly so the broccoli does not burn. Toss in the onion and continue until onion starts to become translucent. Set mixture aside.

Whisk eggs, oregano, basil, garlic, dill, light cream, and celery salt together. When adding the herbs put them in the palm of your hand and rub your hands together over the bowl of eggs releasing them into the mixture to release more flavor.

Add approximately ¼ cup of the broccoli and onion mixture per ramekin then sprinkle about ¼ cup of Italian cheese per ramekin over the broccoli mixture. Add the egg mixture slowly to about ¼ inch from top of each ramekin.

Bake for 30 to 40 minutes. Quiche will rise high in ramekins. Serve immediately.

Serves 8

ZUCCHINI PIE

Ingredients

½ cup diced sweet peppers

½ cup diced onion

½ teaspoon salt

½ teaspoon pepper

½ cup oil

6 whole eggs

1 cup Bisquick

½ cup grated Romano cheese

3 cups thinly sliced zucchini

Directions

Preheat oven to 350 degrees.

Grease a 13 x 9 x 2 inch baking dish. Put all ingredients in a bowl and mix. Transfer to the prepared baking dish. Bake for 30 minutes.

Serves 4 to 6

CHIMICHURRI SAUCE

The sauce is so easy and good; it keeps in the refrigerator for at least a month. The sauce also makes a great marinade or accompaniment for any kind of grilled meat or shrimp.

Ingredients

1 cup packed
fresh Italian parsley

½ cup olive oil

⅓ cup red wine vinegar

½ cup, packed fresh cilantro

2 or 3 garlic cloves, peeled

¾ teaspoon dried
crushed red pepper

½ teaspoon ground cumin

½ teaspoon salt

Directions

Puree all ingredients in processor. Transfer to a bowl. Cover and let stand at room temperature, or make earlier in the day and refrigerate.

Serves 4

RIJSTAFFEL

Fairchild-Muller Curry with Condiments

The Dutch were responsible for importing many curries from India to Java and Bali. This was a popular party dish. Depending on how many servants were used to pass the variety of condiments, it was called a "One boy curry" or "Ten boy curry." Dr. David Fairchild brought this recipe back from his world travels.

It's traditional to have a combination of condiments; sweet, salty, sour and spicy. Use your imagination!

Chopped hard boiled eggs	Canned French-fried onions	Chutney
Chopped sour pickles	Sliced scallions	Unsweetened coconut
Bombay duck	Salted peanuts	Sour cocktail onions
Chopped dried herring	Fried bananas or plantains	Sweet preserved watermelon
Crisp crumbled bacon	Golden raisins	Lime slices

Ingredients

5 pounds cooked, cold lamb, chicken, turkey, or duck

½ cup olive oil, or enough to fill the fry pan up ¼ inch in depth

3 medium onions, thinly sliced

3 tablespoons butter

3 medium apples, sliced, cored, chopped, but not peeled

¼ cup seedless raisins

¼ cup shredded unsweetened coconut

¼ cup fresh lemon or sour orange peel sliced into small thin strips

2 to 4 tablespoons of curry powder

1 pint rich soup stock, chicken or turkey or duck

Directions

Cut the meat into small cubes. Place in a large deep frying pan with ¼ inch of olive oil, and lightly brown the cubes of meat.

In another frying pan brown the onions in butter. Add the sliced apples, raisins, shredded unsweetened coconut, and some fresh lemon or sour orange peel. Cook until slightly browned. Add the curry powder, stir to thoroughly mix, remove from heat, add a little of the stock and scrape all the bits from the bottom and stir to mix.

Add the soup stock into the pan of meat cubes, as well as the onion, and fruit curry mixture. Cover and allow to gently simmer for at least 20 minutes.

Serve with fluffy basmati rice plus any or all of the condiments in small bowls, which can be placed on a lazy susan or passed around the table. This is usually served with ice-cold beer.

Serves 12

MEATS, POULTRY AND QUICHE

HONEYED PORK TENDERLOIN

with Avocado-Peach Salsa

Ingredients

½ cup soy sauce

1 tablespoon sesame oil

2 teaspoons teriyaki sauce

2 garlic cloves, minced

1 teaspoon ginger

1 1-pound pork tenderloin

¼ cup of honey

2 tablespoons brown sugar

4½ tablespoons sesame seeds

Directions

Combine first 5 ingredients in a large shallow dish or heavy duty Ziplock bag. Add pork. Cover and seal 8 hours minimum.

Preheat oven to 400 degrees. Remove pork and discard the marinade. Stir together the honey and brown sugar. Cover pork with the honey mixture and sprinkle with sesame seeds. Place on a lightly greased rack in a roasting pan. Bake for 25-30 minutes, or until the thickest portion registers 170 degrees on a meat thermometer. Serve with Avocado-Peach Salsa.

Serves 2 to 4

Avocado-Peach Salsa

1 cup peeled, diced peaches

1 large tomato, diced

1 to 2 cups diced avocado

1 tablespoon minced red onion

1 tablespoon lime juice

1 teaspoon olive oil

¼ teaspoon salt

¼ teaspoon ground pepper

½ cup diced jicama

Directions

Combine all of the ingredients and chill until ready to serve.

Makes 2½ cups

PORK FRIED RICE

This is good and fast made with leftover pork roast.

Ingredients

2 pounds lean pork, cubed

**1 green pepper,
chopped into large pieces**

3 stalks celery, cut into pieces

2 eggs, scrambled

2 cups rice, cooked

Soy sauce to taste

Directions

Brown pork in a large sauté pan and cook a few minutes. If you are using leftover pork just cube and brown. Add celery, pepper, scrambled eggs and rice. Mix with soy sauce. Cool for a couple of minutes and serve.

Serves 4

SAUERKRAUT & RIBS

Ingredients

**1 32-ounce bag prepared
fresh sauerkraut drained**

**2 pounds country style ribs,
boned and trimmed**

¼ cup brown sugar

**1 10-ounce can
French onion soup, undiluted**

Directions

Preheat oven to 350 degrees. Place the ribs in the bottom of a 9 x 13 x 2 inch casserole dish. Cover with sauerkraut and sprinkle with the brown sugar and top with the French onion soup.

Cover and bake for 3 to 4 hours or until tender. Uncover for the last ½ hour to brown.

Serves 4

SPICY PORK TENDERLOIN

Ingredients

3 pounds pork tenderloin

½ cup soy sauce

6 tablespoons rice vinegar

6 cloves garlic, smashed

¼ cup sliced green onions

2 teaspoons grated fresh gingerroot

1 teaspoon ground red pepper

1 cup water

4 teaspoons cornstarch

Directions

Combine all the ingredients except water and cornstarch, in a Ziploc bag and marinate the pork tenderloin for 24 to 48 hrs.

Preheat oven to 425 degrees. Drain and reserve marinade. Roast the tenderloin for 30 to 40 minutes, uncovered.

Mix the water with cornstarch and add to reserved marinade. Cook until thick over medium heat in a saucepan, then cook 1 minute more. Serve pork tenderloin sliced with the marinade drizzled over top.

Serves 6 to 8

The Montgomery House

TONKATSU

Japanese Pork Cutlet

This is a traditional way to serve pork in Japan.

Ingredients

**1 pound pork tenderloin
or pork shoulder
sliced about ½ inch thick**

Salt and pepper

⅓ cup all purpose flour

**2 eggs beaten together
with 1 teaspoon water**

Panko (Japanese bread crumbs)

Peanut oil

Directions

Remove any excess fat and pound flat the pork slices as you would for veal cutlets. Salt and pepper both sides of cutlets. Dust meat with flour.
Dip in the beaten eggs and water. Cover each cutlet with Panko. Deep fry at 340 degrees until golden brown. The meat will sink to the bottom and then float to the top.

Garnish with cherry tomatoes, watercress, and a lemon wedge.

Serves 4

Tonkatsu Sauce

**4 tablespoons
Worcestershire sauce**

1 tablespoon ketchup

Directions

Mix the sauce ingredients together and serve with the cutlets.

TURKEY AND WILD RICE CASSEROLE

Ingredients

2 cups cooked wild rice

2 cups cooked, cut-up turkey

1 cup chopped celery

1 6-ounce can mushrooms, with juice

1 small onion, finely chopped

1 14-ounce can cream of chicken soup

Salt and pepper to taste

½ cup sherry

⅔ cup nuts, almonds, peanuts or cashews

Seasoned stuffing crumbs, or buttered bread crumbs, for topping over casserole

Directions

Preheat oven to 350 degrees.

Mix all ingredients and put in a large casserole.
Cover with buttered breadcrumbs.
Bake for 45 minutes.

Serves 8

MAXINE'S TURKEY CASSEROLE SUPREME

Ingredients

3½ pounds turkey

1 16-ounce package Pepperidge Farm dressing

1 stick butter, melted

1 can cream of chicken soup, diluted with 1 can chicken broth

1 can cream of mushroom soup diluted with 1 can chicken broth

Directions

Cook the turkey in lightly salted boiling water until tender. Remove turkey from broth and cut into small pieces.

Grease a 13 x 9 x 2-inch baking dish. Mix dressing with melted butter, and set aside ¼ cup for garnish. Put ½ of the dressing mixture into the baking dish. Add the turkey and cover with the chicken soup mixture. Add the other ½ of the remaining dressing mix and cover with the mushroom soup mixture. Sprinkle the top with the ¼ cup reserved dressing mix. Cover and refrigerate overnight.

Preheat the oven to 350 degrees. Remove casserole from the refrigerator 15 to 20 minutes before baking. Uncover and bake for 30 to 40 minutes.

Serves 10

BOUNTY FROM THE BAY

Seafood Dishes

"The Lightkeeper's cottage at Bill Baggs Cape Florida State
Recreation Area was one of the Villagers' most ambitious
projects, spanning four years from 1995-1998.
The project included new museum displays, a theatre, an
archaeological display and interpretive signage."

SEARED SESAME TUNA

with Ginger and Garlic

This recipe is adapted from Jason McClain, chef-owner of 8 ½ Restaurant in Miami Beach, who serves it with asparagus and wasabi-mashed potatoes, and an assertive white wine like 2005 Amisfield Sauvignon Blanc.
Any good quality tuna will work.

Ingredients

¼ cup black sesame seeds

½ cup white sesame seeds

4 6-ounce Ahi tuna steaks, 1 inch thick

4 tablespoons canola oil (divided)

Salt and freshly ground white pepper

Directions

In a shallow dish, combine the two types of sesame seeds and stir to mix. Brush tuna with 2 tablespoons of the oil and season with salt and pepper. Firmly press the sesame seeds into the tuna, coating evenly on all sides.

In a nonstick pan, warm the remaining 2 tablespoons oil over medium-high heat until very hot. Arrange the tuna in the pan, making sure not to crowd, and cook until the white sesame seeds turn golden, 1-2 minutes.

Carefully turn the tuna and cook for another 1 to 2 minutes. The tuna will be rare. If you like it further cooked, place in a preheated 350 degree oven for a few minutes. Transfer the tuna to a cutting board and cut into ¼ inch thick slices.

Serves 4

Ginger Soy Dressing

½ cup soy sauce

½ teaspoon grated fresh ginger

1 teaspoon minced garlic

⅓ cup fresh lime juice

1 tablespoon canola oil

1 tablespoon chopped fresh cilantro

Salt and freshly ground white pepper to taste

Directions

In a small bowl, stir together all the dressing ingredients. Serve immediately alongside tuna. Do not reheat the fish before serving.

MADELEINE'S LOBSTER THERMIDOR

To make this dish even simpler, buy the lobster tails already cooked.

Ingredients

4 tablespoon butter, divided in half

1 cup sliced mushrooms

Chopped scallions

2 lobster tails, boiled and cut into bite size pieces

1½ tablespoons flour

½ cup light cream

¼ cup dry sherry

½ teaspoon dry mustard

¼ teaspoon salt

¼ teaspoon paprika

Dash white pepper

Enough white rice for 2

Directions

In a saucepan, cook mushrooms and scallions in 2 tablespoons butter until tender, about 5 to 7 minutes. Stir in lobster meat. In another saucepan, melt 2 tablespoons butter, add flour, and stir in cream all at once. Cook and stir until thickened and bubbly. Add sherry, dry mustard, salt, paprika, and pepper. Stir into lobster mixture. Serve with white rice.

Serves 2

STUFFED AVOCADOS

with Creamed Lobster

Ingredients

2 ripe medium Florida avocados

1 tablespoon garlic vinegar

½ pound cooked lobster or crabmeat

½ pound sautéed mushrooms

1 cup Cream Sauce

1 tablespoon finely chopped green pepper

1 tablespoon chopped pimiento

Dash of salt

Dash of paprika

¼ teaspoon curry powder

4 tablespoons buttered breadcrumbs

Directions

Preheat the oven to 375 degrees. Cut each avocado in half, take out the seed, and clean up the cavity. Place a little of the garlic vinegar in each half and let the avocados stand for ½ hour.

Meanwhile, combine the rest of the ingredients, except the breadcrumbs, in a bowl and set aside. Pour the vinegar out of the shells and fill them with the creamed lobster sauce. Line a baking pan with wax paper, place the avocado halves on the pan and sprinkle the tops with the buttered breadcrumbs.

Bake for about 15 minutes, or until they are well heated and the tops are brown. Serve with wild rice on the side.

Serves 4

Cream Sauce

3 tablespoons butter

3 tablespoons flour

1 cup milk

Directions

Melt the butter over low heat. Blend in the flour. Stir the milk in slowly. Keep stirring with a wooden spoon until the mixture is creamy. Set aside.

BAKED FISH FILLETS

with a Fresh Tomato Sauce

*A great party dish, and it's especially versatile if you have non-fish
eaters because you can serve the sauce on chicken, too.*

Ingredients

1 Spanish onion

2 shallots

1 pound ripe beefsteak
tomatoes, diced

1 bunch fresh basil or
Italian parsley, chopped

1 6-ounce jar of capers, drained

2 tablespoons lemon juice

1 cup red wine vinegar

1 cup extra virgin olive oil

Salt and pepper to taste

10 6-ounce fillets of white fish

Directions

Slice the onion and shallots. Mix them with the
tomatoes and basil in a glass bowl with the capers,
lemon juice, vinegar, oil, salt and pepper.
Cover tightly and refrigerate for 3 hours.

Preheat oven to 350 degrees. Arrange the fish
fillets on a nonstick baking pan. Layer tomato
mixture on top, making sure that each fillet gets
plenty of oil and vinegar.

Bake for 8 to 14 minutes, or until done.

Serves 10

BAKED SEA BASS

in Miso Sauce

The recipe is very easy, and surprisingly ever-so-tasty.
The white miso imparts a subtle sweet/salty flavor to the fish.

Ingredients

6 tablespoons white miso*

⅓ cup sugar

¼ cup Mirin (sweet Japanese rice wine)*

¼ cup sake

1 pound sea bass or black cod

Sliced green onions or chives for garnish

* Available in the Asian food section of many supermarkets

Directions

Mix all the marinade ingredients in food processor.

Marinate the sea bass at least two hours, or longer. Preheat oven to 375 degrees. Remove the fish from the marinade and bake for 25-30 minutes until flaky. The fish is delicious with jasmine rice.

Serves 3 to 4

EASY GARLIC SHRIMP AND GRITS

Ingredients

1 pound unpeeled, medium fresh shrimp, cooked

3 cups water

1 cup whipping cream

¼ cup butter

1 teaspoon salt

1 cup quick cooking grits

1 cup shredded extra sharp cheddar or other cheese

2 garlic cloves minced

Directions

Peel the cooked shrimp and de-vein. Bring the water, cream, butter and salt to a boil in large saucepan over medium-high heat. Reduce heat to medium, and whisk in grits. Cook, whisking constantly 7 to 8 minutes until mixture is smooth.

Stir in the shrimp, cheese, and garlic and cook 1 to 2 minutes until thoroughly heated. Garnish with white pepper, chives and cooked whole shrimp.

Serves 4

BARBEQUE ROASTED SALMON

Ingredients

¼ cup pineapple juice

2 tablespoons fresh lemon juice

4 6-ounce salmon fillets

2 tablespoons brown sugar

4 teaspoons chili powder

2 teaspoons grated lemon rind

¾ teaspoon ground cumin

½ teaspoon salt

¼ teaspoon ground cinnamon

⅛ teaspoon chipotle powder

Cooking spray

Lemon slices, optional

Directions

Combine the first two ingredients in a Ziploc bag, add the fish, seal, and marinate in the refrigerator for 1 hour, turning occasionally.

Preheat the oven to 400 degrees. Remove fish from the bag and discard the marinade. Combine the sugar and next 6 ingredients in a bowl. Rub over the fish, place in an 11 x 17 x 2 inch-baking dish that has been coated with cooking spray.

Bake for 12 minutes or until fish flakes easily when tested with a fork. Serve with lemon slices, if desired.

Serves 4

Cape Florida Lighthouse

CHILE-GINGER SAUCE

Here's how to use this sauce as an accompaniment for tilapia, but the sauce is highly versatile! It is a recipe from Singapore that is good on rice, noodles, seafood, meat or vegetables. Use it as a dipping sauce for kebabs or spring rolls.

Ingredients

⅔ cup chopped fresh red chiles

10 cloves garlic, peeled

10 slices of peeled fresh ginger

1 tablespoon vinegar
(rice or white)

1 to 2 teaspoons sugar

½ teaspoon salt

4 6-ounce tilapia fillets

salt and pepper, to taste

2-3 tablespoons olive oil

Directions

Put all of the ingredients (except fish) in a blender and process until smooth, adding a few drops of water to thin out a little, if needed.

Salt and pepper the tilapia fillets, then pan fry in about 3 tablespoons olive oil over medium heat (medium-high heat if you like your fish a little crispy). Tilapia fillets are usually rather thin and won't need much cooking, about 2-3 minutes per side. Serve with the sauce spooned over the fish or on the side.

Makes 4 servings

GARLIC SALMON

Great on salmon, but you can use this marinade on any fish.

Ingredients

¾ cup olive oil

1¼ cups soy sauce

2 tablespoons chopped garlic

4 tablespoons dried basil

4 6-ounce salmon steaks,
or any fish you choose

Directions

Mix ingredients and put in a Ziploc bag with the fish for a couple of hours. Preheat the oven to 350 degrees. Remove from the marinade and bake fish until almost cooked, only about 10 minutes, at the most. Finish off by broiling for a few minutes to crisp.

Serves 4

BECKY'S DEVILED CRAB

Here is my favorite dinner party recipe, which was given to me by a dear friend of my mother's when I was only 18. I've served it as my "Number One Company" dish for 40 years! Great breadcrumbs are essential to the dish so don't cut corners.

Ingredients

- 2 cups lump crabmeat
- 2 hard boiled eggs, chopped
- 1 cup real mayonnaise
- 1 beaten egg
- 2 teaspoons finely chopped onion
- 2 teaspoons lemon juice
- 1 teaspoon parsley flakes
- ½ teaspoon Worcestershire sauce
- ½ teaspoon Tabasco
- ¼ teaspoon nutmeg
- ½ teaspoon Dijon mustard
- 3 tablespoons dry sherry
- 1 cup buttered breadcrumbs

Directions

Make the buttered breadcrumbs first. Crumble white bread into 2 cups of tiny pieces and sauté in a half-stick of melted real butter.

Preheat oven to 350 degrees. In a bowl, combine crab (picked over), chopped egg, mayonnaise, beaten egg, and seasonings. Add sherry and half of the sautéed breadcrumbs. Mix well.

Fill scallop shells, or ramekins, and top with the rest of sautéed crumbs. Place shells on a cookie sheet and bake 30 minutes until light and fluffy. Garnish with fresh parsley and lemon wedge.

Scallop shells make a beautiful presentation, but if you don't have any, use ramekins to cook the individual servings in.

Serves 4

BAKED SALMON

with Dill Sauce

Ingredients

2 medium to large tomatoes, diced

1 European cucumber, or 2 regular cucumbers

1 tablespoon Hellmann's mayonnaise, not Miracle Whip

8 ounces sour cream

1 8-ounce cup of fat free plain yogurt

1 1-ounce package of fresh dill

6 6-ounce salmon fillets

Directions

Dice the tomatoes and set aside. Peel cucumbers if using regular cucumbers. Slice cucumbers lengthwise in half. Scoop out the seeds and slice them lengthwise again. Then dice the cucumbers so that the pieces are about the same size as the tomato pieces. Mix with the tomatoes.

Mix the mayonnaise, sour cream and plain yogurt together. Add to the tomato and cucumber mixture. Use about half a package of dill. Cut the dill away from the stems and combine with the tomato and cucumber mixture. Refrigerate for about 3 hours before serving.

Grill or pan sauté the salmon. To serve, place a scoop of the sauce directly on the plate. Put salmon on top of the sauce. Add more sauce to the top of the salmon.

Serves 6

DARU'S MEUNIERE SAUCE

My husband and his friends love this recipe, especially on grouper. It took a while to get it just right, but this one is definitely homemade. There is no salt in the recipe, but I always salt the fish first, to taste. It also helps the Meuniere sauce stay on better. I also use this sauce on my chicken because I am allergic to seafood.

Ingredients

6 sprigs parsley

6 sprigs cilantro

1 shallot

¼ to ½ teaspoon freshly ground pepper mélange (multi-colored peppercorns)

Juice of 1 lemon

½ stick salted butter

Directions

In a small mini Cuisinart, chop parsley, cilantro, shallot and ground pepper mélange, mixing thoroughly. Add the juice of 1 lemon and ½-stick melted but cooled butter and blend some more. You will need to keep the sauce warm so that it doesn't solidify. Spoon over fish just as it's done cooking.

Serves 2

Lantern on the porch of the Lightkeeper's Cottage

SNAPPER FRANÇAISE

Grouper also works very well for this dish.

Ingredients

1 cup all-purpose flour

¾ teaspoon salt

½ teaspoon black pepper

3 large eggs

4 snapper fillets, about 2 pounds

½ cup vegetable oil

½ stick unsalted butter

½ cup dry white wine

½ cup low-sodium chicken broth

3 tablespoons fresh lemon juice
plus 1 whole lemon, thinly sliced

¼ cup chopped fresh
flat-leaf parsley

Directions

In a shallow bowl, stir together flour, ½ teaspoon salt, and ¼ teaspoon pepper. Lightly beat eggs in another shallow bowl. Heat oil in a 12-inch heavy skillet over moderate heat until hot but not smoking.

When oil is hot, dredge the fish, 1 piece at a time, in flour mixture, shaking off excess. Dip floured fish into beaten eggs to coat, letting excess drip off, then fry, turning over once, until golden brown and just cooked through, about 3 minutes total. Transfer to a plate lined with paper towels and keep warm, loosely covered with foil.
Fry remaining fish in the same manner.

Pour off and discard oil, then wipe skillet clean and heat butter over low heat until foam subsides. Add wine, broth, and lemon juice and boil, uncovered, stirring occasionally, until sauce is reduced to about ¾ cup; about 5 minutes.
Stir in parsley and remaining ¼ teaspoon salt and ¼ teaspoon pepper. Place fish back in and simmer 3 or 4 more minutes until done. Top with lemon slices and serve over pasta of your choice.

Serves 4

JUDY'S SEA BASS

If you can find them, sweet blood oranges add a pretty color to the dish.
Yum! Yum! Yum!

Ingredients

Olive oil

1 clove of garlic, minced

1 ½ pound fillet Chilean sea bass, skinned and washed

1 lime, juiced

1 to 2 oranges, juiced

1 large leek, thinly sliced, round wise

3 to 4 shallots finely sliced and diced

½ ruby red grapefruit, juiced, optional

Parsley dried, to fill your hand; if using fresh parsley use a heaping handful

1 teaspoon Coleman's Dry Mustard

1 teaspoon paprika

¼ to ½ cup sake

4 tablespoons butter or Benecol, melted

Directions

Preheat oven to 350 degrees. Drizzle 2 tablespoons olive oil in a glass 8 x 11 x 2 inch baking dish. Sprinkle the garlic in the bottom of the dish. Place skinned and washed fish in the middle of the pan. Pour the juice from the lime and oranges (or grapefruit) over the fish. Sprinkle the sliced leeks and diced shallots over the top of the fish.

Top with the parsley, then spread the Coleman's mustard and paprika over. Add the butter to the top of the fish. Pour sake over everything and bake the seasoned fish, uncovered, for 40 minutes or until a fork separates the fish easily.

Serves 4

SEAFOOD CAKES

These have a very southwestern taste with a lot of cilantro in the dressing. They're great with hot garlic bread. I like them best made with crab so try it as an alternative to the shrimp and scallops. Both the cakes and Garlic-Cilantro Dressing can be made ahead of time, and just bake and serve at the last minute.

Ingredients

1 shallot, minced

¼ cup minced red bell pepper

6 ounces peeled cooked shrimp

10 ounces sea scallops

1¼ cups Panko
(Japanese bread crumbs)

2 tablespoon Parmesan cheese

1 egg, beaten slightly

2 tablespoon whipping cream

⅔ cup cilantro

4 tablespoon chopped chives

½ teaspoon salt and pepper

Flour

1 beaten egg

1¼ cups Panko

2 tablespoon Parmesan cheese

¼ cup oil

Directions

In a large skillet sauté shallots and red bell pepper until soft. Set aside. Chop shrimp and scallops into pea size pieces and place in a mixing bowl. Add Panko, the beaten egg, whipping cream, 1 tablespoon Parmesan, the cooked red pepper and shallot, cilantro, chives, and salt and pepper to taste.

Form into 8 (2½ to 3 inch) patties. Dust cakes with flour. Dip in egg. Combine the additional 1¼ cups Panko with the 2 tablespoons Parmesan, and dip the cakes in the mixture to coat. Fry cakes until lightly brown, 3 to 4 minutes per side over medium heat. Recipe can be done the day before up to this point.

When ready to serve bake at 375 degrees for 10 minutes.

Makes 8 cakes

Garlic-Cilantro Dressing

1 small shallot, diced

½ cup chopped cilantro

1 small clove garlic, chopped

1 Serrano chili, seeded and chopped

¼ cup white wine vinegar

¼ teaspoon salt and pepper

1 teaspoon Dijon mustard, optional

½ cup olive oil

Directions

To make the dressing, process all the ingredients in a blender. The dressing may also be made the day before serving.

Presentation for four:

Salad greens for 4	While the seafood cakes are baking, arrange salad greens on four plates. Top greens with two seafood cakes. Drizzle on dressing. Garnish with sliced tomato and thinly sliced red onion.
2 ripe tomatoes	
8 thin slices red onion	

SNAPPER

in a Wine and Cheese Sauce

Ingredients

2 eggs

6 ounces white wine

½ pound cheddar cheese, diced

⅓ pound butter

2 pounds snapper fillets, boned, and cut into pieces

Directions

In a blender combine the eggs, 4 ounces of the white wine, and the cheddar cheese. Blend until liquefied. Set aside.

In an ovenproof skillet, melt the butter. Add the snapper pieces and simmer on low heat until white on both sides. Add remainder of the white wine. Pour blended cheese, wine, and egg sauce on top of the snapper. Place the skillet under the broiler until a light brown crust is formed. Serve in the skillet on a breadboard at the table.

Serves 4

ORANGE DIJON SALMON

An easy and elegant meal for company.

Ingredients

6 tablespoons Dijon mustard

9 tablespoons soy sauce

9 tablespoons orange olive oil

9 tablespoons virgin olive oil

1½ teaspoons minced garlic

4 6-ounce center-cut salmon fillets with skin

Directions

Combine the marinade ingredients and pour into a glass-baking dish. Add the salmon, turn to coat and marinate for 1 to 3 hours, turning occasionally.

Remove salmon from marinade. Preheat broiler or grill. Broil or grill the salmon, skin side down, 5 inches from heat until golden, about 3 minutes. Turn the fillets and broil or grill for 4 minutes, or until the skin is crisp and the fish is not quite cooked through. Transfer to a plate and serve.

Serves 4

SHRIMP HARPIN

Double the recipe and you have a great meal for 20.
A green salad and rolls with butter finishes out the meal.

Ingredients

2½ pounds raw shrimp,
shelled, deveined

1 tablespoon lemon juice

3 tablespoons olive oil, divided

¾ cups uncooked rice

2 tablespoons butter

½ green pepper, minced

½ onion, minced

1 teaspoon salt

¼ teaspoon pepper

¼ teaspoon mace

½ to ¾ teaspoon cayenne pepper

1 can tomato soup, undiluted

1 cup heavy cream

½ cup dry sherry,
not cooking sherry

1 cup slivered almonds, divided

Directions

Early in the day thaw and cook the shrimp in a skillet in oil until just pink. Place contents of skillet in a 2-quart casserole and sprinkle with lemon juice; refrigerate.

Cook rice and let it sit while covered. Refrigerate if you are not using right away.

About an hour before serving preheat oven to 350 degrees. Set aside 8 to 10 shrimp for garnish and ½ cup of the almonds.

In a large pan, sauté green pepper and onion for 5 minutes in oil. Add rice, salt, pepper, mace, cayenne pepper, soup, cream, sherry, and ½ cup of almonds. Mix well and gently blend in the shrimp. Put everything back in the casserole dish. If shrimp is a little watery drain off some of the oil and water before mixing.

Bake covered, with foil, for 30 minutes; then top with remaining shrimp and almonds and bake uncovered for about 15 minutes until bubbly and slightly browned on top.

Serves 8

CAMARONES AL AJILLO

Shrimp in Garlic Sauce

This simple recipe is very Spanish, but while in Spain shrimp is generally served with its shell on; in Cuba it was most often peeled and de-veined before cooking. Serve it with white rice.

Ingredients

1 cup Spanish olive oil

16 large shrimp, shelled and de-veined

10 garlic cloves, peeled and cut into thick slices

¼ cup freshly squeezed lime juice

1¼ teaspoons salt

½ teaspoon freshly ground pepper

1 tablespoon chopped parsley

Directions

Heat the oil in a large, heavy skillet over medium-high heat until it is fragrant. Add the shrimp and garlic, and sauté until the shrimp turns pink, about 3 minutes.

Add the limejuice, salt, and pepper. Sauté for about 2 minutes more, being careful not to overcook the shrimp. Transfer the shrimp to a serving dish and sprinkle them with chopped parsley.

Serves 4

SHRIMP MOUTARDE

Ingredients

2 tablespoons butter

2 tablespoons chopped scallions

1 teaspoon garlic, chopped

1 tablespoon lemon juice

1 tablespoon Dijon mustard

½ cup dry white wine

½ cup whipping cream

1 pound medium to large shrimp, shelled and cleaned

Directions

Sauté scallions and garlic in butter in a large sauté pan. Add lemon juice, mustard and white wine. Reduce for 15 seconds. Add cream and stir. Bring to a boil. Add shrimp. Do not crowd. Remove the shrimp with a slotted spoon as they soon as they are done. After the shrimp have cooked continue stirring sauce until it thickens. Pour sauce over shrimp. Serve over rice with a green vegetable.

Serves 4

PAPAYA-MANGO SALSA

Use with grilled or pan fried red snapper, grouper or other firm white-fleshed fish fillets. And, if someone is not a fish eater, it's also great on chicken.

Ingredients

3 tablespoons sugar

1½ tablespoons vinegar

Pinch red chili pepper flakes

Pinch cumin

1 medium papaya, seeded, peeled and diced

1 cup mango, peeled and diced

½ small red onion, diced

3 tablespoons red bell pepper, diced

2 tablespoons cilantro, chopped

Directions

Mix sugar, vinegar, chili flakes and cumin until sugar dissolves. Fold in remaining ingredients. Cover and refrigerate until ready to serve.

Makes 2½ cups

Dormer window in the Lightkeeper's Cottage

SCALLOP STEW

"Sailing to Maine on a Yacht"

Can be served as a stew with toast or on a bed of rice.

Ingredients

5 slices bacon

½ pound large sea scallops

1 onion, chopped

1 cup vegetable or chicken broth

1 cup white wine

4 large potatoes, cut into 1-inch cubes

1 cup heavy cream

3 ears of corn, kernels cut off

Directions

Sauté the bacon in a deep saucepan. Remove the bacon and then sauté the sea scallops until slightly golden brown. Do not overcook. Remove the scallops and set aside with the bacon.

Sauté the chopped onion in the same pan until transparent, at a low heat, and then add the vegetable or chicken broth, white wine, potatoes and the heavy cream. Cover and cook over low heat until soft, stirring frequently. Add the corn kernels to the pot, then when the pot starts to bubble again, add the scallops, and crumble the bacon over the soup. Stir and serve.

Makes 6 cups

SASSY SIDETRACKS

Vegetables and Grains

"Using Villager grant funds, the doors to the historic
mini-train tunnel were replaced at Virginia Key Beach Park."

THE VILLAGERS

ASPARAGUS

with Ginger-Orange Vinaigrette

A citrus-y take on asparagus, courtesy of Whole Foods Market, that really hits the spot. You can also try grilling or roasting the asparagus.

Ingredients

1 tablespoon finely chopped fresh ginger

½ teaspoon finely grated orange peel

2 tablespoons orange juice

2 teaspoons white wine vinegar

⅓ teaspoon soy sauce

¼ teaspoon salt

¼ teaspoon freshly cracked black pepper

3 tablespoons extra virgin olive oil

1 pound asparagus, washed, tough ends snapped off

Directions

Whisk together ginger, orange peel, orange juice, vinegar, soy sauce, salt and pepper. Slowly whisk in olive oil until an emulsion forms. Set aside.

Steam asparagus until just tender, about 5 minutes. Drizzle vinaigrette over warm asparagus and serve.

Serves 4

LEMON RICE

Ingredients

1 garlic clove

2 cups chicken broth

2 tablespoons butter

½ teaspoon salt

1 cup basmati rice

1 tablespoon grated lemon rind

1 teaspoon dried dill, to taste

Directions

Slightly mash the garlic clove using the flat side of a knife. In a large saucepan, stir together the garlic, broth, butter and salt; bring to a boil over high heat. Stir in the rice; reduce heat to low and cook, covered, for about 20 minutes or until the broth mixture is absorbed and rice is tender. Remove and discard the garlic; stir in the lemon rind (and dill, if using) using a fork.

Serves 8

MARTA'S CUBAN BLACK BEANS

Ingredients

1 pound black beans

10 cups water

1 large green pepper, chopped

⅔ cup olive oil

1 large white onion, chopped

4 cloves garlic, minced

1 green pepper, diced

4 teaspoons salt

½ teaspoon black pepper

¼ teaspoon oregano

1 bay leaf

2 tablespoons sugar

2 tablespoons vinegar

2 tablespoons white wine

2 tablespoons olive oil

Directions

Wash the beans well in cold water. Leave overnight in 10 cups of water and the chopped green pepper. The next day, place the water, beans, and green pepper in a pot and cook for 45 minutes.

In a separate frying pan, heat the oil; add the chopped onion, garlic, and the second green pepper. Take a cup of the beans that have been partly cooked and mash them and add them to the onion, garlic, and green pepper mixture. Sauté for a few minutes. Pour everything back into the pot with the rest of the beans and add the salt, pepper, oregano, bay leaf, and the sugar. Bring to a boil, stirring occasionally, and then simmer for one hour.

Add the vinegar and white wine. Increase the heat to medium and cook for another hour, so that the beans are well cooked. Before you serve, add the 2 tablespoons of olive oil, and stir well. Serve with white rice.

Serves 6

CORONADO BROWN RICE CASSEROLE

Ingredients

¼ cup butter, unsalted

1 cup chopped onion

4 cups cooked brown rice (Uncle Ben's brand brown rice cooks better)

2 cups sour cream, low fat

1 cup cream-style cottage cheese, low fat

1 large bay leaf

½ teaspoon salt

⅛ teaspoon pepper

2 4-ounce cans chopped green chilies

2 cups grated sharp Cheddar cheese

Directions

Preheat oven to 375 degrees. In a large pan, sauté the onion in butter until golden. Remove from heat and stir in cooked rice, sour cream, cottage cheese, bay leaf, salt, pepper, chopped chilies, and most of the cheese. Spoon the mixture into a lightly greased 3-quart baking dish. Sprinkle remaining cheese on top.

Bake uncovered for 30 minutes. This can be made a day or two ahead and refrigerated. Bring to room temperature before baking.

Serves 8

CARROTS
with Horseradish Glaze

Ingredients

1 16-ounce package baby carrots

1¼ teaspoons salt, divided

3 tablespoons butter

⅓ cup honey

2 tablespoons prepared horseradish

Directions

Cook carrots and 1 teaspoon of the salt in boiling water to cover in a large saucepan for 15 minutes or until tender, and drain.

Melt the butter in the saucepan over medium-high heat; stir in honey, horseradish, and remaining ¼ teaspoon salt. Add carrots, and cook, stirring gently for 5 minutes.

Serves 4

CAULIFLOWER-TOMATO AU GRATIN

Ingredients

2 packages frozen cauliflower

1 cup grated American cheese

2 medium onions

5 sprigs parsley

3 tablespoons butter

1 20-ounce can tomatoes

1 bouillon cube

1 tablespoon sugar

1 teaspoon salt

Dash of pepper

3 tablespoons dry breadcrumbs

Directions

Preheat oven to 350 degrees. Cook the cauliflower as directed on the package. Drain and toss the cauliflower in ¾ cup of the grated cheese.

Chop onions and parsley fine and cook in the melted butter until onions are limp. To this add the tomatoes, a bouillon cube, sugar, salt, pepper, crumbs, and cook slowly for about 5 minutes. Put half the mixture in the bottom of a greased 2-quart casserole, add the cauliflower and top with remaining sauce. Sprinkle remaining cheese over the surface. Cover, bake for 15 minutes. Uncover, and bake 15 minutes longer.

Serves 8 to 10

JALAPENO CORN CASSEROLE

A great side dish with mashed potatoes, and is perfect with holiday dishes.

Ingredients

2 16-ounce cans shoe peg white corn or frozen white corn

1 8-ounce package cream cheese with chives & onions (or other similar seasonings)

3 to 4 fresh jalapeno peppers, seeded and chopped

Salt to taste

Directions

Preheat oven to 350 degrees. Combine all of the ingredients in a covered casserole. If you use frozen corn adjust the salt. Bake covered for about 30 minutes.

Serves 6 to 8

COLLARD GREENS

With Almonds

Umeboshi vinegar is made from the ume plum and adds a wonderful sweet tangy flavor to greens. You can find it in the health food section in grocery stores.

Ingredients

1 pound collard greens, rinsed, thick stems removed

¼ cup almonds, slivered and blanched

2 tablespoons sesame oil

½ teaspoon Amleoshi vinegar or Umeboshi vinegar

1 tablespoon apple cider vinegar

1 small clove garlic, minced

Directions

In a skillet, toast almonds over medium heat until golden in color, about 1 or 2 minutes. Set aside.

Fill the sink with cold water to wash the greens. Put greens in the sink and swish around. Greens will float to top of water and dirt and grit will drop to the bottom of the sink. Shake water off the greens.

Layer 3 collard leaves. Roll into a cylinder and slice crosswise into thin strips. Repeat until all are sliced. In a large pan filled with a steamer basket, bring 2 inches of water to a boil over high heat. Add greens. Cover and steam for 4 minutes.

In a small bowl whisk sesame oil, both vinegars and garlic until blended. Toss greens with dressing and garnish with toasted almonds. Serve hot.

Serves 6

For Auntie Janie's Classic Collard Greens:

Leave out the sesame oils, vinegar and almonds. After washing and slicing greens, pour olive oil over the bottom of a skillet, and sprinkle salt in it. Add the greens, and then turn on the heat to high. Once sizzling, turn greens up from bottom with wooden fork. Do this for about two minutes, until greens are dark and glistening.

ELLEN'S "AU ROTTEN" POTATOES

Ingredients

6 red potatoes, medium sized

¾ cup grated Parmesan cheese, to taste

¾ cup milk, to taste

Salt and pepper to taste

Havarti or Swiss cheese, as desired

Directions

Preheat oven to 375 degrees. Boil potatoes (with skins on) so that they are soft enough to grate, but not too soft that they will fall apart. Allow them to cool and then peel. Grease a casserole dish with butter or margarine.

Grate the potatoes into the casserole dish. Blend in the Parmesan cheese and milk. Add the milk slowly while blending so as not to make the dish too wet. The consistency should be wet enough that you can stir easily but not soupy. Add salt and pepper to taste. Place strips of white cheese on the top, for additional flavor and appearance. Bake for approximately 20-25 minutes to heat thoroughly and melt the cheese.

Serves 6

The mini-train at Virginia Key Beach

HUNGARIAN NOODLES

This dish goes great with beef tenderloin and Caesar salad.
You can easily double this recipe and use a 9 x 13-inch pan.

Ingredients

2½ cups fine egg noodles, uncooked

1 cup sour cream

1 cup cottage cheese

¼ cup chopped onion

1 tablespoon poppy seeds

Parmesan cheese, grated

Directions

Preheat oven to 375 degrees.

Cook noodles. Mix the next four ingredients. Top with the Parmesan cheese. Bake in a buttered 8 or 9-inch square pan for 30 minutes.

Serves 6 to 8

SCARLETT'S ACORN SQUASH

Ingredients

1 large acorn squash

1 8-ounce can crushed pineapple

⅓ cup Craisins

½ cup brown sugar

1 teaspoon ground cinnamon, optional

Directions

Preheat oven to 350 degrees. Cut squash in half, microwave on high, flesh side down in ¼-inch water for approximately 7 minutes or until tender.

Remove seeds and excess membrane. Carefully scoop out the squash pulp from both halves and mix with the rest of ingredients. Add to a sauté pan and cook on top of the stove for 10 minutes, stirring often. Replace mixture into squash shells and bake at 350 degrees for 15 minutes until hot and bubbly.

Serves 2 to 4

ROASTED APPLES AND PARSNIPS

A recipe courtesy of Whole Foods Market that combines sweet apples and earthy parsnips, which makes a perfect accompaniment to roast pork, chicken or turkey. Great for the holidays!

Ingredients

1 ½ pounds parsnips, peeled

1 pound Gala or Braeburn apples, cored and peeled

½ teaspoon salt

¼ teaspoon black pepper

2 tablespoons extra-virgin olive oil

1 tablespoon fresh sage, coarsely chopped

Directions

Preheat oven to 475 degrees, and place oven rack in upper third of oven.

Cut parsnips lengthwise into quarters and then into 2-inch pieces. Cut apples into quarters and then into 2-inch pieces. Toss parsnips and apples with salt, pepper, olive oil, and sage. Spread in one layer in a large shallow baking pan. Roast, turning occasionally, until parsnips and apples are tender and browned, about 20 to 25 minutes.

Serves 4

APRICOT RICE

Ingredients

3 to 4 cups of jasmine rice

½ cup dried apricots, diced

3 to 4 tablespoons finely chopped fresh dill

Salt

Directions

Cook rice according to package directions. Remove from heat when done and add diced apricots. Let sit for five minutes for apricots to take on some of the rice's moisture, then add dill. Add salt to taste.

Serves 8 to 10

KAY'S TOMATOES AND ARTICHOKE HEARTS

Ingredients

1 36-ounce can organic whole plum tomatoes

1 14-ounce can artichoke hearts

½ cup onion, finely chopped

2 tablespoons shallots, finely chopped

¼ pound butter

½ teaspoon basil

1 or 2 tablespoons balsamic vinegar, or to taste

1 to 2 tablespoons sugar

Salt and pepper to taste

Directions

Preheat oven to 325 degrees. Grease a shallow casserole bowl. Drain the tomatoes and artichokes, then rinse the artichokes in water and quarter them.

Sauté the onion and shallots in the butter until tender. Add the tomatoes, artichokes and basil, heat for 2 or 3 minutes, stirring gently. Season with the balsamic vinegar, sugar, salt and pepper. Turn into the prepared casserole and bake for 10 to 15 minutes or until the vegetables are heated through.

Serves 6 to 8

SAUTÉED BABY BOK CHOY

Ingredients

6 fresh baby bok choy

3 tablespoons extra virgin olive oil

1 garlic clove, diced

1 tablespoon sherry or other white wine

Salt, to taste

Fresh ground pepper, to taste

Directions

Cut baby bok choy in half lengthwise. Heat olive oil in sauté pan. Place bok choy cut side down over medium-high heat. Add garlic. Sprinkle with salt and pepper. Turn the bok choy when it begins to get a light golden brown color. Repeat on other side. Add a splash of sherry or white wine. Remove from heat and arrange on a platter.

Serves 8 to 10

WHOLE ROASTED CAULIFLOWER

with Lemon Caper Dressing

The olive oil will caramelize the florets, which are perfectly complimented by the lemon caper dressing.

Ingredients

1 2-pound head of cauliflower, green leaves discarded

2 tablespoons extra-virgin olive oil

1 teaspoon salt

1 tablespoon fresh lemon juice, or to taste

1 tablespoon drained small capers

¼ teaspoon black pepper

¼ cup extra-virgin olive oil

2 cups loosely packed fresh flat-leaf parsley sprigs

Directions

Put oven rack in the middle position and preheat oven to 450 degrees. Lightly oil a 9-inch square-baking dish.

Core the cauliflower, leaving the head intact, then discard the core and put the cauliflower head in the pan. Drizzle 2 tablespoons of the olive oil over the top of the cauliflower and sprinkle with ½ teaspoon of the salt. Bake until tender, about 1 to 1¼ hours. Transfer to a serving dish.

While baking, whisk together the lemon juice, capers, pepper, and remaining ½ teaspoon salt in a small bowl. Whisk in the additional ¼ cup olive oil.

Place the cauliflower on a serving dish, surround with the parsley and drizzle the dressing over everything.

Serves 8

PORTUGUESE MASHED POTATOES

Cooking the potatoes in the milk and bay leaves gives a subtle flavor that makes these potatoes very special.

Ingredients

2 pounds potatoes, peeled and cut into 1 inch cubes

2 large bay leaves

1 cup chicken or vegetable stock

1 cup milk

1 teaspoon salt

1 teaspoon fresh ground pepper

¼ cup (½ stick) butter, cut into chunks

Directions

Place potatoes and bay leaves in a 4-quart saucepan. Add the potatoes, bay leaves, stock, and milk. Add water, if necessary, to cover the potatoes. Bring to a boil. Reduce heat to low, cover and simmer 15 to 20 minutes or until potatoes are fork tender. Watch the pot so that the milk does not cause the liquid to boil over.

Drain the liquid into a bowl and reserve ½ cup of the liquid. Return the potatoes to the pan. Remove the bay leaves. Add the salt and pepper. Mash with a potato masher, gradually adding the butter and reserved stock until you reach the desired consistency. Serve immediately.

Serves 4

BOSTON STYLE POTATO PANCAKES

Always make more than one batch, because one is never enough!

Ingredients

1 pound of potatoes, about 2 cups shredded with a large grater

1 egg

1 small onion, finely grated

1 tablespoon flour

½ tablespoon salt

Dash of pepper

¼ teaspoon baking powder

Olive oil or other light oil for frying

Directions

Peel potatoes and if not using immediately cover with cold water. Beat egg. Shred potatoes using large holes of the grater and then press out moisture on a towel or in a sieve.

In a large bowl, combine grated potatoes with egg, onion, salt, pepper, flour and baking powder. Mix well. Heat ¼ inch of oil in a heavy frying pan. Spoon 2 to 3 tablespoons of potato mixture into oil and press firmly with the back of a spoon or spatula for form thin pancakes.

Fry until golden brown. Taste first batch to see if more seasoning is needed. As each batch is removed add more oil if necessary and let it heat. Drain pancakes on a paper towel and transfer to a rack above a cookie sheet. Keep warm in a 225 degree oven until ready to serve.

Serve with sour cream and/or applesauce.

Makes about 10

CROWD PLEASERS

Feeding the Multitudes

ITALIAN STRATA

Ingredients

2 packages crescent rolls

½ pound sliced deli salami

½ pound sliced deli provolone

½ pound sliced deli boiled ham

6 large eggs

1 cup grated Parmesan cheese

2 12-ounce jars roasted red peppers, drained

Directions

Preheat oven to 350 degrees. Coat a 13 x 9 x 2-inch glass baking dish with non-stick cooking spray. Unroll 1 package of the crescent rolls and use to line the bottom of the prepared baking dish. Pinch seams together with fingers.

Cover rolls with ½ of the salami, provolone, and ham. Lightly beat together the eggs and Parmesan cheese. Pour ½ of the mixture evenly over the top of the meats. Top with the roasted peppers. Repeat layering with remaining salami, cheese, ham, egg mixture and roasted peppers. Top with remaining package of crescent rolls.

Cover dish with foil and bake for 30 minutes. Uncover and bake 30 minutes more. Cool for 1 hour and cut into squares and serve.

Makes 32 squares

TROPICAL BUFFALO WINGS

Ingredients

50 chicken wings

1 bottle of your favorite mojo

1 cup Crystal hot sauce

½ cup butter

Directions

Marinate wings in the mojo for 24 hours.
Grill the wings over medium high heat until done.
Melt butter in a pan and add the hot sauce.
Pour the mixture over the wings before serving.

Makes 50 wings

SMOKED FISH DIP

Although you can extend the amount of fish with the cream cheese and sour cream, be careful not to overpower the fish with any other ingredients.

Ingredients

3 cups smoked fish

8 ounces cream cheese, softened

½ small Vidalia onion, diced

½ cup chopped celery

2 tablespoons sour cream

Directions

Strip away skin, bones and bloodline on the smoked fish fillet, if needed. Shred the fish in the food processor. Blend in cream cheese to bind. Chop onions and celery and mix. Add one or two spoonfuls of sour cream to smooth out texture.

Serve with crackers, and top with a dash of Crystal Hot Sauce, Tabasco or Louisiana Hot Sauce to spice it up.

Serves 16

PITA CHEESE CRISPS

Ingredients

2 sticks butter

2½ cups grated Cheddar cheese

2½ cups grated pepper jack cheese

1 cup grated Parmesan cheese

1½ rounded tablespoons minced fresh garlic

¾ teaspoon Worcestershire sauce

1 teaspoon paprika

½ teaspoon cayenne pepper

9 6-inch pita breads

Directions

Preheat oven to 350 degrees. In a food processor, combine the cheeses, butter, garlic, Worcestershire, paprika, and cayenne. Split each pita open into two flat disks. Spread with the cheese mixture, and cut each disk into 8 wedges.

Place the wedges on an un-greased cookie sheet or parchment paper, and sprinkle with additional paprika for color. Bake 11-13 minutes. May be served warm or at room temperature. They also freeze well.

Makes about 72 wedges

SNAPPY BITES

This is a great party food and they freeze well if you want to make them ahead of time. I make them for road trips - instant party!

Ingredients

1 cup butter, softened

2 cups sifted flour

3 ounces sharp cheddar cheese, grated

½ teaspoon salt

½ teaspoon cayenne pepper

2 cups Rice Krispies

Directions

Preheat oven to 350 degrees. Cut butter in flour until mixture resembles coarse corn meal. Mix in cheese, salt and cayenne pepper. Add Rice Krispies and mix. Pinch off in small pieces (about a teaspoon size, too large and the bites will be too doughy) and form balls, flattening slightly. Bake on greased cookie sheet at 350 degrees for 15 minutes, or until just turning brown at the edges.

Makes about 50

CAPONATA DIP

Make this the day before and gently reheat just before serving.

Ingredients

⅔ cups olive oil

1 large eggplant, unpeeled, cut into ½ inch cubes

1 zucchini, diced

4 cloves garlic, crushed

1 onion, chopped

2 tablespoons capers

2 16-ounce cans Italian-style tomatoes, chopped, slightly drained

1 tablespoon red wine vinegar

1 teaspoon sugar

½ teaspoon dried Italian herbs

Salt and pepper, to taste

Directions

Heat olive oil in a very large skillet. Sauté the eggplant for about 5 minutes or until soft. Add the remaining ingredients. Cook over medium heat for about 25 minutes or until most of the liquid evaporates.

Serve with crackers, pita bread, sliced French baguette, etc.

Serves 14

HEARTY HODGEPODGE SOUP

This soup can easily be doubled for larger groups, or divide into smaller servings and freeze for a later date. Perfect for unexpected guests!

Ingredients

1½ pounds ground meat; use a mix of beef and turkey

¾ cup chopped onion

1 clove of minced garlic

3 15-ounce cans of your favorite minestrone soup

1 31-ounce can of pork and beans

1½ cups of chopped celery

1 tablespoon Worcestershire sauce

½ teaspoon dried oregano

3 cups water, or more if needed

Directions

Cook ground meat, onion, and garlic until meat is browned. Drain grease. In a large pot, combine meat with soup, beans, celery, Worcestershire sauce, oregano and water. Simmer covered for at least 20 minutes.

Serves 12 to 14

LISA AND MAXINE'S CHICKEN SALAD

This is a great luncheon salad!

Ingredients

1⅓ cups mayonnaise

4 tablespoons apple cider vinegar

2 teaspoons salt

8 cups cooked, cubed
chicken or turkey

2 cups minced green peppers

4 teaspoons grated Vidalia onions

1⅓ cups slivered,
toasted almonds

4 cups halved,
seedless red/green grapes

2 cups sliced celery

2 heads Romaine lettuce

Directions

In a large bowl, combine mayonnaise, vinegar and salt with a fork. Add chicken and remaining ingredients except romaine; toss well; cover and refrigerate for at least a couple of hours to let flavors meld.

When ready to serve, arrange Romaine leaves on a platter and top with chicken salad.

Serves 18 to 20

TORTELLINI SALAD

This salad is best served after it has been chilled for a half hour.

Ingredients

3 7-ounce packages of tortellini, cooked (tri-color looks best)

1 can artichoke hearts, quartered

½ cup sun dried tomatoes

1 cup olives, optional

⅓ cup pine nuts

1 large tomato, sliced

Fresh basil

1 red pepper, diced

1 green pepper, diced

1 tablespoon of Dijon mustard

1½ teaspoons oregano

3 tablespoons balsamic vinegar

¾ cup extra virgin olive oil

Directions

Mix together all the ingredients. Add a dash of pepper, 3 tablespoons balsamic vinegar and ¾ cup extra virgin olive oil. Refrigerate before serving.

Serves 12

The Coral Gables Congregational Church tower.

KAY'S BLACK BEAN & PAPAYA SALAD

This is all give or take a bit, so have fun. Feel free to substitute ingredients like blueberries for the black beans. Add more color by using green onion or lettuce. It is a great recipe that is fun to tweak.

Ingredients

1 or 2 15-ounce
cans of black beans, drained

1 large papaya, 10 or more inches
in length, or 2-3 medium red
papayas, peeled, seeded
and cut into ½ to 1 inch slices

½ small red onion, thinly sliced
or a few green onions, sliced

4 stalks of celery chopped

½ cup coarsely chopped
mint leaves

Directions

Combine the black beans, papaya and onion and celery. Toss all together. Pour the dressing over the salad and toss again. Cover with plastic wrap and refrigerate for at least 30 minutes. Add mint, toss again, and serve about room temperature.

Serves 14 to 16

Ginger-lime Dressing

6 tablespoons fresh lime juice

1 tablespoon minced fresh
ginger, but I've used jarred

1 tablespoon honey,
or more to taste

4 tablespoon olive oil

1 teaspoon salt

¼ teaspoon freshly
ground pepper

Directions

Combine the lime juice, ginger and honey. Whisk in olive oil and season with salt and pepper. Set aside.

LIME-PEAR JELL-O SALAD

Ingredients

1 large can pears

1 large package lime Jell-O

1 8-ounce package cream cheese

1 pint whipping cream

½ cup chopped toasted almonds, walnuts, or pecans; optional

Directions

Drain pear juice and heat in a small pan; pour over the Jell-O. Stir until dissolved. Mash drained pears with a fork. Soften cheese with a little of the pear juice. Add mashed pears and softened cream cheese to the Jell-O.

Let cool, then fold in the whipped cream. Sprinkle chopped nuts on top of mold if desired. Refrigerate for next day.

Serves 12

CRANBERRY JELL-O

Ingredients

1 pint sour cream

2 3-ounce packages raspberry Jell-O

1 15-ounce can whole cranberry sauce

1 package frozen raspberries

1½ cups liquid using juice from the raspberries and water

Directions

Drain raspberries, saving the juice, and set fruit aside. Heat cranberries and the 1½ cups of liquid. Pour heated liquid over Jell-O and stir to dissolve. Thicken slightly in the refrigerator.

Whip sour cream and raspberries together and add to Jell-O mixture.

Pour into mold and refrigerate.

Serves 12

WARM HAM AND CHEESE SANDWICHES

This recipe is from the first "Three Rivers Cookbook"- a series of very good Pittsburgh cookbooks. Two Villagers tweaked the recipe and made over 2000 of these little sandwiches for the 1996 Christmas House Tour. They were a hit!

Ingredients

½ pound butter, softened

3 tablespoons
honey Dijon mustard

2 tablespoons poppy seeds

½ teaspoon Worcestershire sauce

1 medium onion, grated

2 packages finger dinner rolls,
24 rolls each

1 pound thinly sliced honey ham

6 slices Jarlsberg cheese,
medium thickness

Directions

Mix the first 5 ingredients. Slice the rolls cross-wise, and carefully open them as if opening a book. Spread mixture on both sides of roll. Place ham and cheese evenly to edges of the bottom sections, then replace top section. Put rolls on an aluminum tray. Wrap in foil and heat 15 minutes at 400 degrees. These may be frozen, and then defrosted before heating.

Makes 24 mini sandwiches

Variations
The basic recipe can be adapted to whatever you have in your pantry and refrigerator!

• Try Pillsbury biscuits, both the Grands and the small biscuits (refrigerated rolls) will work.

• Try a variety of fillers: shaved ham, cooked bacon, shredded cheddar cheese, shredded mozzarella cheese, small pieces of tomato.

CHICKEN CASSEROLE

*A cinch for large groups! You can make this the night before,
then bake on the day of your event. It is always well received.*

Ingredients

1 cup butter or margarine

2 packages Stove Top
Chicken Stuffing mix

4 large chicken breasts,
cooked and cubed

Pam, or other baking spray

2 cans cream of chicken soup

2 cups sour cream

2 cups chicken broth

Directions

Preheat oven to 375 degrees. Spray a 9 x 13 x 2-inch
glass casserole dish with Pam. Melt butter in a large
skillet. Add the stuffing mix, and stir to coat.

Put ½ of stuffing mix into casserole. Add chicken on
top. In a bowl, mix the soup, sour cream, and broth.
Pour the sauce over the chicken. Top with remainder
of stuffing mix. Bake approximately 1 hour.

Serves 12 to 14

FROGMORE STEW

*This is the famous "low-country boil" from the coastal regions of the south, and
is considered a southern specialty. It is traditionally served on a newspaper-
covered picnic table, eaten with your fingers, and shared with family and friends.*

Ingredients

5 quarts water

½ cup Old Bay Seasoning

4 pounds small red potatoes

2 pounds kielbasa or other
sausage in 1½-inch pieces

6 ears fresh corn, halved

4 pounds unpeeled,
large fresh shrimp

Cocktail sauce, 3 sticks butter,
salt and fresh ground black pepper

Directions

Heat water and Old Bay to a rolling boil in a large
covered stockpot. Add potatoes, and return to a
boil, uncovered, for 10 minutes. Add sausage and
corn and boil 10 minutes or until potatoes are
tender. Add shrimp and cook 3 to 4 minutes until
shrimp turn pink. Drain and serve with cocktail
sauce for the shrimp, butter for the corn, and
seasonings for the potatoes.

Serves 12 to 14

FEEDING THE MULTITUDES

SPINACH STRATA

This is a great dish to make for the holidays. The recipe makes two dishes;
so freeze one for later use. Be sure to defrost before baking.

Ingredients

3 packages chopped spinach,
defrosted and well drained

4 tablespoons chopped onions

2½ cups shredded
cheddar cheese

1¾ tablespoons
fresh lemon juice

12 ounces sliced mozzarella

2 medium cans tomatoes,
sliced and drained

1 4-ounce can sliced mushrooms

10 eggs, slightly beaten

6 cups milk

3 teaspoons salt

1 teaspoon oregano

¼ teaspoon garlic powder

1 cup grated Parmesan cheese

2 loaves thinly sliced
white bread, crusts removed

Directions

Butter the bottom of two 9 x 13 x 2-inch pans. Mix
together the spinach, onions, cheddar cheese, and
lemon juice. Cover the bottom of the two pans with
some of the bread slices and spread the mixture
on top. Add a second layer of bread to each pan,
then the mozzarella, tomatoes and mushrooms.
Add a third layer of bread. Mix together the eggs,
milk, salt, oregano, garlic powder, and Parmesan
cheese. Pour egg mixture over all and sprinkle with
generous amount of Parmesan cheese. Refrigerate,
covered, overnight.

Preheat oven to 325 degrees. Bake uncovered
for 1 hour and 15 minutes. You may sprinkle with
additional Parmesan before serving.

Serves 20

LEG OF LAMB

with Roasted Tomato-Olive Sauce

*Have the butcher butterfly the lamb and cut the bones into 3-inch pieces.
Make the sauce the day before when you marinate the meat. The day of
the party all you'll have to do is grill the lamb and heat the sauce.*

Marinade

1 cup olive oil

6 tablespoons fresh lemon juice

4 tablespoons Dijon mustard

2 tablespoons chopped garlic

2 tablespoons chopped fresh
rosemary

2 teaspoons black pepper

2 6-pound legs of lamb, boned,
butterflied and trimmed, bones
reserved

Directions

Marinate the lamb in a large glass baking dish
overnight. The next day, heat the barbecue grill to
medium-high heat. Grill lamb about 12 minutes per
side for medium-rare. Slice lamb and arrange on a
platter. Pass sauce separately.

Serves 14 to 16

Roasted Tomato-Olive Sauce

7½ pounds ripe plum tomatoes,
blanched, peeled, cut in half,
deseeded

1¼ cups olive oil

lamb bones cut into 3-inch pieces

2 cups shallots, chopped

3 tablespoons plus
1 teaspoon minced garlic

1⅓ cups chopped Kalamata olives
or other brine-cured
black olives

3 tablespoons drained capers

2 tablespoons plus 2 teaspoons
chopped drained anchovy fillets

2½ teaspoons
chopped fresh rosemary

Directions

Preheat oven to 400 degrees. Combine tomatoes and
olive oil in a large baking pan. In another baking
pan spread out the lamb bones. Roast tomatoes until
they begin to brown. Roast the bones until brown
and fat is released, about 50 minutes. Cool.

Remove tomatoes from the oil and chop. Pour oil
from the roasted tomatoes pan into a heavy large
skillet. Add 2 tablespoons of the drippings from
the roasted bones and add to the oil in the skillet.
Discard the bones. Heat the pan over medium-
high heat. Add the shallots and garlic and sauté
3 minutes. Add the chopped tomatoes and all
remaining ingredients and stir until heated through.
Cover and refrigerate. Before serving, warm sauce
over low heat or serve at room temperature.

BAKED BEANS

with Apples

Ingredients

1 pound dried navy beans

1 pound salt pork, diced

**3 tart apples, peeled,
cored and coarsely chopped**

1 medium onion, chopped

½ cup packed dark-brown sugar

½ cup molasses

1 tablespoon dry mustard

3 tablespoons vinegar

½ teaspoon pepper

½ teaspoon salt

Directions

Rinse and pick over the beans; cover with water and soak overnight. Drain and place in a large Dutch oven with water to cover by one inch. Bring to a boil, reduce heat and simmer until skins begin to burst and beans are tender, about one hour.

Preheat oven to 300 degrees. Add the salt pork, apples, onion, brown sugar, molasses, mustard, vinegar, salt and pepper to the pot of beans.

Bake, covered, for 6 hours. Add hot water if the beans become too dry while baking.

Serves 12

HASH BROWN POTATO CASSEROLE

This is great for all those potluck occasions.
You can make it a bit healthier by using non-fat and low-salt ingredients.

Ingredients

1 32-ounce bag of frozen hash browns, cubed or shredded

¼ cup melted butter

8 ounces shredded cheddar cheese

1 cup chopped onion

1 pint sour cream

1 can cream of chicken soup

1 teaspoon garlic powder

1 cup corn flakes

¼ cup melted butter to pour over the corn flakes

Directions

Preheat oven to 350 degrees.

Partially thaw potatoes. In a large bowl, mix together the ¼ cup butter, cheddar cheese, chopped onion, sour cream, soup, and garlic. Stir the potatoes into the mix. Spread into a greased 13 x 9 x 2-inch pan. Sprinkle with slightly crushed corn flakes and pour butter over the top.

Bake covered for 1 hour, then take the cover off and bake for another 15 minutes.

Serves 12

SWEDISH BROWNIES

Ingredients

2 sticks butter, melted

2 cups sugar

2 eggs

2 cups flour

Dash salt

2 teaspoons almond extract

⅓ cup slivered almonds

Directions

Preheat oven to 350 degrees.
Grease a 10 x 15 x 2-inch pan.

Melt butter and cool. Combine butter, sugar and eggs. Mix well. Add flour, salt and almond extract. Pour into the prepared pan and sprinkle with almonds. Bake for 20 to 30 minutes, or until lightly brown. Cool completely. Recipe freezes well.

Makes 60 squares

MARINER'S RUM PUNCH

The thermal fluid cooler is the big orange cooler that you see on the sidelines of football games or on the back of work trucks. I had to stop making this recipe because my friends were drinking too much of it!

Ingredients

3½ liters Bacardi Rum

2 quarts fresh orange juice

2 quarts guava juice

2 quarts pineapple juice

6 cups lime juice

3 cups Cointreau

1 cup Grenadine syrup

4 tablespoons Angostura Bitters

Directions

Place all ingredients in a large thermal fluid cooler and add a 5 lb. block or bag of ice. Chill and serve.

Note: The fruit pulp will settle to the bottom and stop up the flow of the punch. Periodically use a long handled spoon to mix the punch. You can also just take the top off and use a ladle.

Makes 50 8-ounce servings

THE BARNACLE'S BRANDY PUNCH

A recipe from Jessie Worth Munroe, second wife of Commodore Ralph Munroe.

Ingredients

1 pound superfine sugar

1 fifth lemon juice

1 fifth cognac

2½ fifths sauterne wine

Fresh mint

Directions

Place sugar in gallon jug and add lemon juice. Shake until sugar dissolves, then add cognac and mix. Top with sauterne or any good white wine. Mix well and chill. When time to serve, pour over a large piece of ice in a bowl. Garnish with mint.

Mixture may be stored in ½ gallon bottles until ready to use. Add one bottle at a time to punch bowl.

Serves 20 to 25

OSCAR'S CHAMPAGNE PUNCH

Oscar, the Chef at the Waldorf Astoria and a friend of my grandfather, Joseph Ulrich, gave this recipe to my mother, and after that, it has been a family tradition for three generations of Whitehurst women.

Ingredients

4 quarts of wine, champagne, or dry sauterne

2 quarts of 7-Up

1 small can of frozen orange juice, thawed, or fresh orange juice

1 can chunk pineapple, or fresh

1 jar maraschino cherries, drained

Directions

To make a decorative ice ring or block, fill a container shape of your choice halfway with water and freeze. After frozen, put seasonal flowers over the ice, and finish filling with water to the top; freeze again.

Combine in a punch bowl and put block, ring or cubes of ice in the bowl.

If a non-alcoholic punch is needed, you may substitute fresh grapefruit juice for the wine.

Serves 50

STRAWBERRY TEA

Ingredients

1½ quarts boiling water

3 large tea bags

½ cup sugar or Splenda

1 6-ounce can frozen lemonade concentrate

1 10-ounce package frozen strawberries

Directions

Make the tea, brewing for 4 minutes.
Stir in the sugar, lemonade and strawberries.

Serve over ice and garnish with fresh strawberries, or pour over a frozen ice mold.

Makes 2 quarts

FEEDING THE MULTITUDES

THE DEVIL MADE ME DO IT

Desserts

"The recent restoration of Courtroom 6-1 in the Dade County Courthouse included the replication of the original lighting and wall sconces, made possible by a grant from the Villagers."

THE VILLAGERS

PINEAPPLE BREAD PUDDING

This is a Jamaican recipe that can be easily doubled for a crowd.

Ingredients

¼ pound sweet butter

1 cup sugar

1½ teaspoons vanilla

½ teaspoon cinnamon

4 eggs

10 slices white bread, crust cut off and cut into cubes

1 20-ounce can crushed pineapple with juice

¼ cup golden raisins

Directions

Preheat oven to 350 degrees. Cream the butter and sugar, and add the vanilla and cinnamon. Beat in the eggs. Combine the bread, pineapple and raisins; add to the sugar mixture and pour in a buttered 1½-quart baking dish. Bake for 45 minutes or until done.

Delicious served warm or at room temperature.

Serves 8

STRAWBERRY SORBET

Ingredients

1 pound ripe strawberries, cleaned, tops removed, pureed

1¼ cups sugar

2 cups water

1 tablespoon lemon juice

1 teaspoon vanilla

Directions

Boil sugar and water 2 minutes. Add strawberry puree and lemon juice and vanilla.

Pour in a shallow glass dish. Freeze for about two hours, stirring every 30 minutes to break up the crystals. If it becomes too hard, scrape into a food processor and pulse, do not puree. Re-freeze until ready to use.

You may also make this in an ice cream maker. Just follow the manufacturer's directions.

Serves 4

SISTER JANE'S EASY APPLE CAKE

My sister gave this to me in the late 1950s. It's so good and so easy. Plus it never fails to garner raves. I took it to a funeral reception. A man came to me at the end and inquired about who brought this sweet cake...he had gone back for it 5 times!

Ingredients

1¾ cups sugar

1 cup cooking oil

3 eggs

2 cups un-sifted flour

1 teaspoon cinnamon

1 teaspoon baking soda

4 apples, pared and sliced as for pie

½ cup chopped nuts.

Confectioner's sugar for dusting

Directions

Preheat oven to 350 degrees. Grease a 9 x 13 x 2 inch pan. Beat sugar, oil, and eggs in an electric mixer. Sift together flour, cinnamon, and baking soda. Stir the dry ingredients into the wet ingredients by hand. Stir in the apples and nuts. The batter will be stiff. Bake for 1 hour. Cool in pan. Sprinkle with confectioner's sugar.

Serves 12

OATMEAL CRISPIES

Ingredients

1 cup shortening

1 cup brown sugar

1 cup granulated sugar

2 eggs, well beaten

1 teaspoon vanilla

1 teaspoon salt

1½ cups flour

1 teaspoon baking soda

2 cups oatmeal

1 cup Rice Krispies

½ cup chopped nuts

1 small package chocolate chips

Directions

Cream the shortening and sugars. Add the eggs and vanilla and beat well. Add the salt, flour and baking soda. Mix well. Add the oatmeal, Rice Krispies, nuts and chocolate chips.

Fold everything together. Drop by the teaspoon-full on cookie sheet and bake for about ten minutes or until nicely brown.

Makes 60 cookies

CHOCOLATE CHIP RUM CAKE

Ingredients

1 box Duncan Hines Butter Recipe Golden Cake Mix

1 small box instant vanilla pudding

1 stick butter, room temperature

½ cup salad oil

4 teaspoons vanilla

4 tablespoons dark rum

1 cup light sour cream

4 eggs

1 cup chocolate chips

Directions

Preheat oven to 325 degrees. Mix together all of the ingredients, except the chocolate chips. Batter will be slightly lumpy. Stir in chocolate chips last. Pour into a greased Bundt pan. Bake for 55-60 minutes.

Serves 12

GRANDMOTHER BOLLIN'S POUND CAKE

Ingredients

2 sticks unsalted butter, room temperature

3 cups sugar

6 eggs

3 cups sifted flour

1 cup whipping cream

2 teaspoons vanilla

1 teaspoon almond extract, optional

2 tablespoons bourbon

Directions

Cream together the butter and sugar until light and fluffy. Add eggs one at a time and beat for 2 minutes each. Continue beating and add flour and whipping cream a little at a time alternating and ending with whipping cream. Add vanilla, almond, and bourbon and mix only until blended. Turn the batter into a greased and floured tube or Bundt pan. Put in a COLD oven and bake at 300 degrees for 1½ hours.

Serves 10 to 12

OATMEAL SPICE CAKE

Ingredients

1½ cups boiling water

1 cup quick cooking oats

½ cup butter or margarine

1 cup brown sugar

1 cup white sugar

2 eggs

1 ½ cups flour

1 teaspoon baking soda

1 teaspoon cinnamon

1 teaspoon nutmeg

½ teaspoon salt

Directions

Preheat oven to 350 degrees.
Grease a 13 x 9 x 2-inch baking pan.

Pour boiling water over oats and mix well.
Cream butter and sugars thoroughly. Beat in eggs.
Stir in soaked oatmeal. Sift together flour and the
remaining ingredients. Stir into the oatmeal mixture.

Turn into the prepared pan and bake for 30 to 35
minutes. Cool in the pan.

Spread with the topping and broil until golden,
about 2 minutes or less.

Serves 8

Topping

¼ cup brown sugar

½ cup sugar

1 cup flaked coconut

1 cup chopped nuts

6 tablespoons butter or margarine

¼ cup light cream

¼ teaspoon vanilla

Directions

Combine first 6 ingredients in a medium saucepan
and heat until bubbly. Stir in vanilla. Broil the cake
for 2 minutes after applying the topping.

PUMPKIN SQUARES

This is an all-time Villager favorite!

Ingredients

1 8-ounce package cream cheese, softened

1 16-ounce box powered sugar

3 eggs beaten

1 stick butter, soft

1 teaspoon vanilla

1 can pureed pumpkin (small)

A little cinnamon and nutmeg, to taste

½ cup chopped pecans, optional

Directions

Preheat oven to 350 degrees. Beat the filling together, except for pecans and pour over the crust. Sprinkle the chopped pecans over the batter, if desired.

Bake for 40 to 45 minutes or until top is golden brown but not burned. Cut into squares, serve warm or cold with whipped cream.

Serves 24

Crust

1 box yellow cake mix

1 stick butter, melted

1 egg

Directions

To make the crust, mix the yellow cake mix, butter and egg together and pat into a well-greased and floured 9 x 13-inch pan.

SQUARE MOUSSE PIE

Also known as Chocolate Mousse Pie

Ingredients

5 7-ounce almond Hershey bars

16 marshmallows

½ cup milk

½ pint heavy whipping cream

Ready-made graham cracker crust or ready-made pie shell, pre-baked.

Directions

Melt the first three ingredients together in a double boiler. Cool well. Whip the heavy cream. Add the stiffly whipped cream to the cooled mixture. Pour into the graham cracker crust or pie shell. Refrigerate.

Serves 6 to 8

OLD CHARLESTON POST OFFICE CHEWY CAKE

Serve with a scoop of vanilla ice cream and caramel sauce.

Ingredients

½ cup butter, melted

2 cups, packed light brown sugar

2 eggs

½ teaspoon salt

2 cups sifted flour, sift before measuring

1 teaspoon vanilla extract

1 cup pecans

Directions

Preheat oven to 325 degrees. Combine the butter and brown sugar in a mixing bowl and beat well. Beat in the eggs one at a time. Add the salt and sifted flour, mixing well. Stir in the vanilla and pecans.

Pour into a greased and floured 9 x 13-inch cake pan. Bake for 30 minutes or until the cake tests done. Cut into bars.

Makes 24 bars

SHERRY POUND CAKE

In Memory of Dottie Zinzow.
This recipe was found handwritten inside her cookbook.

Ingredients

1 Package Duncan Hines Yellow cake mix

1 Package Instant Vanilla pudding mix, regular size

4 eggs beaten

½ teaspoon nutmeg

½ cup Wesson oil

1 cup of sherry

Directions

Preheat oven to 350 degrees. Mix all ingredients 5 to 10 minutes with electric beater. Spray a Bundt pan or 9 x 13-inch pan with Pam. Do not flour. Pour mixture into pan and bake for 45 to 50 minutes. Let cool and dust with powdered sugar.

Serves 12 to 24

SWEDISH APPLE CAKE

This is a very special dessert. It takes time to make, but it is worth it.

Ingredients

1 egg

⅔ cup sugar

½ cup butter, melted and cooled

1 cup sifted all-purpose flour

1½ teaspoons double action baking powder

½ cup sugar

2 medium cooking apples (McIntosh or Gala)

1 tablespoon butter, melted

Cinnamon, optional

Directions

Pre-heat oven to 350 degrees. Grease and flour an 8½ or 9-inch round Pyrex baking pan. Beat egg until light. Gradually beat in the sugar. Add the melted and cooled butter. Sift together flour and baking powder and fold into the mixture. Spread batter evenly in pan.

Peel and core apples, cut in quarters lengthwise. Cut each quarter in 4 slices. Roll slices in ½ cup sugar and arrange in a wheel on top of the batter. Spoon melted butter over the apples. Sprinkle cinnamon over top if desired.

Cover baking pan tightly with aluminum foil. Bake for 25 minutes. Remove foil and continue baking 15 to 20 minutes. Serve warm as is or add whipped cream or ice cream if desired.

Serves 8

KEY LIME PIE

The most popular South Florida dessert! It's great just like it is, or top it with a dollop of whipped cream and a small slice of key lime for garnish.

Ingredients

Graham cracker crust

1 can sweetened condensed milk

½ cup fresh squeezed key lime juice

3 egg yolks

Directions

Preheat oven to 350 degrees. Combine the condensed milk, key lime juice, and egg yolks. Whisk together until smooth. Pour into the piecrust. Bake for 7-10 minutes, let cool and then refrigerate before serving.

Serves 6

RUBY-FLECKED FLORENTINE COOKIES

Ingredients

2 cups sliced almonds, divided

½ cup unsalted butter

1 cup sugar

½ cup dried cranberries

½ cup golden raisins

1½ teaspoons finely shredded orange peel

½ cup Golden Syrup (such as Lyle's) or light-colored corn syrup

¾ cup all-purpose flour

Directions

Line baking sheets with parchment paper or a nonstick baking liner (Silpat) or generously grease them. Set aside.

Process ½ cup of the almonds in a blender or food processor fitted with a metal blade until they are finely ground. Melt the butter over low heat in a medium saucepan. Remove the saucepan from the heat and add, one at a time, the sugar, cranberries, raisins, orange peel, syrup, and flour, stirring after each addition. Stir in the finely ground almonds and the remaining sliced almonds.

Using 1 tablespoon dough per cookie, roll mixture into balls. Dough will be sticky; moistened hands will help. Place 3 inches apart on cookie sheets; cookies will spread.

Bake 12 minutes or until golden brown. Cool on sheets 10 minutes; transfer to wire racks to cool completely. Store in an airtight container at room temperature up to 4 days (on humid days, cookies may lose their crispness when stored at room temperature). Or store in freezer up to one month.

Makes 45 cookies

MARLIN'S GINGERSNAPS

Ingredients

¾ cup Crisco

1 cup sugar

1 egg

4 tablespoons molasses

2 cups flour

1½ teaspoon baking soda

½ teaspoon salt

1 teaspoon each cinnamon
ground ginger, ground cloves

⅓ cup granulated sugar,
to roll the gingersnaps in

Directions

Cream first four ingredients with an electric mixer. Combine the flour, baking soda, salt and the spices, and stir into molasses mixture. At this point you can refrigerate the dough for easier handling or freeze it to make the cookies at a later time.

Preheat the oven to 325 degrees. Place the granulated sugar in a plate and roll the dough into walnut sized balls. Roll the balls in the sugar and place about 2 inches apart on an un-greased cookie sheet. Bake for 10 to 12 minutes or until the tops of the cookies begin to "crack." Remove from the oven and allow the cookies to remain on the sheets for a minute or so to firm up. Remove the cookies to cooling racks.

Note: Do not over bake if you want the cookies to be chewy. They will still have good flavor, but they will become very hard if left in the oven too long. They also freeze very well.

Makes about 4 dozen

NO-BAKE KEY LIME PIE

Ingredients

1 graham cracker crust pie shell

1 can Eagle brand sweetened condensed milk

½ cup Key lime juice

1 8-ounce carton Cool Whip

Directions

Slowly combine the condensed milk with the key lime juice. Once mixture is completely combined, fold in the Cool Whip. Pour into the piecrust and refrigerate for several hours.

Serves 6

ORANGE SLICES BAR COOKIES

A special Southern heirloom recipe. Most recipes call for orange candy slices.

Ingredients

¼ cup all purpose flour, for dusting

2 tablespoons butter

1 cup brown sugar

2 eggs, beaten

1 tablespoon water

1 teaspoon vanilla

1 cup all purpose flour

½ teaspoon baking powder

1 cup pecan or walnuts

1½ cup orange slices cut into small pieces

Directions

Pre-heat the oven to 325 degrees. Dust the nuts and orange slices with a little flour. Cream the butter and sugar. Add the beaten eggs and mix well. Add water, vanilla, flour, baking powder, nuts, and orange slices.

Bake for 30 minutes in a 9 x 13-inch pan. Cut into squares while hot.

Makes 28 squares.

Variation: Add ½ cup coconut, and 1 cup oatmeal to the batter

POTATO CHIP COOKIES

A nostalgic favorite from the 1960s when we didn't worry about cholesterol. The recipe can be easily doubled for a big party.

Ingredients

2 sticks margarine or butter

½ cup sugar

1¾ cups flour

1 teaspoon vanilla

½ cup potato chips, crushed.

Directions

Preheat oven to 350 degrees. Cream the butter and sugar. Add flour and vanilla. Fold in the chips. Make into small balls and place on an un-greased cookie sheet. Bake for 15 minutes and let cool. Sift confectioner's sugar over the top, if desired.

Makes 50 cookies

MINI "WATERMELON" WEDGES

The lime and strawberry filling look like little watermelons; it makes a great presentation for parties! A fun recipe to make with kids as well.

Ingredients

8 Persian limes cut in half

1 cup vanilla yogurt

2 cups frozen whole strawberries, thawed and pureed

mini-chocolate chips, to taste (for "watermelon seeds")

Directions

Stir together yogurt, strawberries and mini-chocolate chips. Chill while you hollow out the lime halves, leaving rinds intact. Fill with yogurt/strawberry/chip mixture and freeze for 8 hours. Balance on mini muffin tins. Cut frozen lime halves in half with a serrated knife to make mini "watermelon" wedges.

Yields 28 to 32 wedges

Fan detail in Courtroom 6-1.

LEMON MOUSSE

with Berry Puree

When you grate citrus rind for zest, be sure to only grate the colored skin, not the bitter white pith just underneath the skin.

Ingredients

2 envelopes unflavored gelatin

4 large lemons, grate the rind for zest, then juice to get ½ cup juice

10 eggs, separated

1½ cups superfine sugar, divided into 1 cup plus ½ cup

1½ cups heavy cream

Pinch of salt

Directions

In small saucepan, sprinkle gelatin over lemon juice and let soften for 5 minutes. Meanwhile, beat the egg yolks until they are light yellow and gradually add 1 cup superfine sugar, beating all the while. Stir in the lemon rind.

Melt the gelatin mixture over low heat until the gelatin dissolves; do not let it boil. Let cool for a few minutes. Drizzle the gelatin mixture over the egg yolks and mix well. Set aside to cool thoroughly.

Beat the cream until stiff and fold it gently into the cooled egg yolk mixture. Beat the egg whites with salt until stiff. Gradually add the ½ cup superfine sugar, beating constantly. Fold egg whites into the cream mixture. Transfer into serving bowl, cover, and refrigerate for at least 3 hours before serving. If you would like, top this with a berry puree.

Serves 8

Note: If you can't find superfine sugar whirl some granulated sugar in a food processor or spice grinder for 2 minutes.

Berry Puree

Raspberries, blueberries, blackberries, and/or strawberries (Fresh or frozen)

Granulated sugar to taste

Directions

Use any combination of berries you can find. Puree in a food processor or blender and add sugar to taste.

SARA'S PAPER BAG PIE

Sara Severud gave this recipe to Emily Savage (the first Villager president) when Emily represented Florida in the Mrs. America Contest in 1963. The judges thought the pie was fantastic and ate the whole thing! Sara was a creative, wonderful cook, and measurements are left to your individual taste. Use more of the ones you like, but be sure to include the nutmeg, which gives this pie its distinctive flavor.

Ingredients

6 to 8 peaches or apples, peeled and sliced into wedges

½ cup sugar

2 tablespoons flour

½ to 1 teaspoon cinnamon

½ to 1 teaspoon nutmeg

Directions

Preheat oven to 425 degrees. Shake enough peaches or apples in a paper bag with the dry ingredients to fill the unbaked piecrust. Squeeze the juice of ½ lemon on top.

Put the whole pie in a paper bag and seal by folding over ends several times and staple or paper clip. Bake for 1 hour.

Serves 6

Pie Crust

1 cup flour

2 tablespoons Crisco

3 tablespoons cold water

Directions

Cut Crisco into flour and add water to moisten. Form into a ball and let rest in the refrigerator for 1 hour. Roll out and put into a pie plate.

Topping

½ cup sugar

½ cup flour

1 stick butter

Directions

To make the topping, combine the ingredients with a pastry cutter to make a coarse meal and sprinkle over the fruit mixture.

WENDY'S PAVLOVA

This recipe is from New Zealand, and is an easy dessert perfect for company young and old alike. If you can't find superfine sugar, whirl granulated sugar in a food processor for 2 minutes.

Ingredients

6 large egg whites at room temperature

1¼ cups castor sugar

1 teaspoon vanilla

1 teaspoon cornstarch

1 teaspoon malt vinegar

Directions

Preheat oven to 400 degrees. Place parchment paper on a cookie sheet. You may need to put a small amount of oil on corners of cookie sheet to hold paper down. Draw a circle on the parchment paper using an 8-inch cake pan.

Beat egg whites until very stiff in a metal or glass bowl using an electric beater.

Gradually beat in sugar by adding sugar a teaspoon at a time. Using a spatula, fold in vanilla, cornstarch, and then vinegar. Pile the mixture in the shape of a small cake on the baking paper (mixture will spread when cooked). Make a small depression in center of mixture so that you can add fruits and whipped cream after baking when serving.

Put Pavlova in pre-heated oven and turn the oven off. Leave in oven until the oven is cold.

To serve, put fresh fruit (strawberries, kiwi, peaches, etc.) in center and top with whipped cream or ice cream if desired.

The outside of the Pavlova will be crisp and the interior creamy so whipped cream or ice cream is really not necessary. However, fresh fruits are always delicious.

Serves 8

BANANA SPLIT PIE

Ingredients

1 stick of butter

2 cups graham cracker crumbs

½ cup sugar

1 large package instant vanilla pudding

2 cups milk

8 ounces cream cheese, room temperature

4 ripe bananas, peeled and sliced

1 large can well drained crushed pineapple

1 large container of Cool Whip

½ cup drained, chopped Maraschino cherries

1 cup pecan pieces

Directions

To make the crust, melt the butter and mix with the graham cracker crumbs and sugar. Put into a glass 9 x 3 inch dish and pat down.

Beat together the pudding, milk and cream cheese for 10 full minutes to thicken. Spread in the pan. Add bananas over the filling. Mix together the pineapple and Cool Whip and spread over the bananas. Top with the cherries and pecans.

Refrigerate overnight, spoon out, and enjoy!

Serves 12

BLUEBERRY CRISP

Ingredients

8 cups blueberries, washed and drained

1 cup of flour, divided in half

½ cup sugar

Juice from one lemon

¾ cup dark brown sugar

½ cup cold butter cut in pieces

Directions

Preheat oven to 350 degrees. Toss the blueberries with ½ cup flour, sugar and lemon juice. Spread evenly in a deep-dish pie pan, pressing down lightly. In a small bowl, mix together the remaining flour and brown sugar; add butter. Mix butter into the dry ingredients so that it looks like coarse crumbs. Spread crumbs over blueberries.

Bake for 10 minutes. Reduce heat to 325 degrees and bake until crumbs are brown, about 1 hour. Serve warm. Top with ice cream or whipped cream if desired.

Serves 8

PEACH COBBLER

Ingredients

1 stick of butter

3 cups peaches, sliced, fresh or canned

¾ cup sugar, use ¼ cup if using canned peaches

Pinch cinnamon

Dash nutmeg

¾ cup sugar

¾ cup flour

2 tsp baking powder

Pinch of salt

¾ cup milk

Directions

Preheat the oven to 350 degrees. Melt 1 stick of butter in a deep baking dish. To make the filling, toss the sliced peaches with the ¾ cup sugar, cinnamon and nutmeg.

To make the batter, stir the other ¾ cup sugar, flour, baking powder, salt and milk into a bowl. Pour the batter into the melted butter but do not stir. Then pour the peaches on top of the batter, but do not stir. Bake for 1 hour.

Serves 4 to 6

MANGO BREAD PUDDING

This is a very easy and different company dessert. Lay out all the ingredients and mix them together right before you sit down to dinner. It will be ready to serve after your main course. Delicious with honey ice cream.

Ingredients

½ pound brioche or egg bread, diced small

1 cup fresh ripe mango, diced small

2 large eggs, add an extra if they are smallish

2 cups milk

½ cup sugar

½ tablespoon vanilla

1 cup heavy cream, whipped right before serving, or ice cream

Directions

Preheat oven to 350 degrees. Butter 8 2-ounce ramekins, or you may use one medium size soufflé dish. Whisk eggs in large bowl to blend. Add milk, sugar, and vanilla; whisk to blend well. Stir in bread and mango. Pour mixture into prepared ramekins. Bake pudding uncovered until puffed and golden, about 20-30 minutes. Cool slightly. Serve warm with whipped cream.

Serves 8

BOHEMIAN COOKIES

Ingredients

1 cup softened butter

1 10-ounce package
semi-sweet chocolate chips

1¼ cup powdered sugar

1½ cups all-purpose flour

1 cup chopped pecans

1 teaspoon vanilla

Directions

Preheat oven to 250 degrees. Chop the chocolate chips and set aside. Beat together butter and sugar thoroughly. Beat in vanilla. Stir in flour by hand until completely combined. Stir in the nuts.

Form into small balls about 1 inch in diameter. Place on an un-greased cookie sheet 1½-inches apart. Bake for 45 minutes, or less for chewier cookies.

Makes 36

PRALINE PUMPKIN PIE

Ingredients

1½ cups solid packed pumpkin

1 cup granulated sugar

2 eggs, slightly beaten

1 teaspoon ground cinnamon

½ teaspoon salt

¼ teaspoon ground ginger

¼ teaspoon ground cloves

¼ teaspoon ground nutmeg

1½ cups undiluted Carnation
evaporated milk

1 9-inch unbaked pie shell

½ cup pecans

⅓ cup firmly packed
brown sugar

3 tablespoons butter
or margarine melted

Directions

Preheat oven to 350 degrees. In a large bowl, combine pumpkin, granulated sugar, eggs, cinnamon, salt, ginger, cloves and nutmeg. Gradually add evaporated milk; mix well and pour into the un-baked pie shell. Bake for 30 minutes.

Meanwhile, in a small bowl, combine pecans, brown sugar and butter. Remove pie from oven; and sprinkle the pecan mixture over the top. Continue baking 20 to 25 minutes or until a knife inserted near the center comes clean. Cool completely on a wire rack. Filling will firm up while cooling.

Serves 6

CUBAN FLAN

There is a special flan pan that has a cover that will clamp down on the pan while it bakes, but you can use a round metal cake pan and cover tightly with foil.

Ingredients

1 cup white sugar

5 large eggs

1 cup whole milk

1 can of condensed milk

1 teaspoon vanilla

Directions

Preheat the oven to 350 degrees. Set a teakettle to boil water for the water bath. In a small saucepan, using medium heat, slowly dissolve the sugar until it turns into a caramel liquid. Pour this mixture into a 9-inch round pan, covering bottom and sides. Set the pan aside and let it cool completely before pouring in the custard mixture.

In a blender slowly beat the eggs, whole milk, condensed milk and vanilla.

Pour into the pan (once sugar has cooled). Cover tightly, place the pan inside a larger pan to make the water bath, pouring in enough hot water to come halfway up the flan pan. Bake for 45 minutes, or until a knife inserted in the custard comes out clean.

Let cool completely before refrigerating for at least 4 to 6 hours. To serve, run a knife around the edge of the pan and invert onto a serving platter. Pour all of the caramel from the mold over the top of the flan.

Serves 8

ORANGE FLOAT

A recipe from Jessie Worth Munroe, second wife of Commodore Ralph Munroe.

Ingredients

⅓ cup water

2 lemons, juiced, pulp reserved

1 cup sugar

6 oranges, peeled and sliced
into round slices, pith and seed
removed

3 egg whites

6 tablespoons sugar

¼ teaspoon vanilla

Directions

Place the lemon juice, lemon pulp, sugar and water
in a small saucepan. Over high heat, gently swirl
the pan until sugar comes to a boil and the liquid is
clear and unclouded.

Cover the pan and boil for a minute or two; the
steam will wash sugar crystals off the sides of the
pan. Uncover the pan and boil until the bubbles
begin to thicken and the temperature reaches
220 degrees and makes a sugar syrup. Take the
syrup off the stove and strain. Let cool.

Place the prepared oranges in a wide shallow bowl.
Pour the cold syrup over the sliced oranges and
let soak for at least an hour.

Beat the egg whites until foamy. While beating,
gradually add the sugar until the mixture is shiny
and holds stiff peaks. Fold in the vanilla.

Serves 4

Note: *If you don't want to have raw egg whites, place
the meringue a serving spoon at a time down into
boiling hot water, lifting them out carefully with a
skimmer when cooked, and then lay them on the float.*

CARAMELIZED APPLE TARTS

*A fancy yet simple dessert that can be
prepared ahead and baked during dinner.*

Ingredients

**7 apples, peeled, cored,
sliced ⅛-inch thick**

¾ cup sugar

½ stick butter

¼ teaspoon salt

**1 tablespoon Calvados
or Applejack**

**2 tablespoons freshly squeezed
lemon juice**

**1 sheet of a 17.3-ounce package
frozen puff pastry**

Caramel Ice Cream for serving

Directions

Sauté the apples with the sugar, butter, salt,
Calvados, and lemon juice over medium heat. Stir
gently until they are soft and completely cooked.
Let them cool to room temperature.

Remove one sheet from the package and allow to
come to room temperature before unrolling onto
a lightly floured board. Cut into 5-inch squares.
Transfer the squares to a baking sheet, leaving
room around each square. Cover and re-freeze for
at least an hour.

Preheat the oven to 375 degrees. Thaw the pastry
squares at room temperature about 15 minutes,
until they soften. Place ½ cup of the sautéed apples
in the middle of each square. Fold the corners of
the pastry over the apples.

Bake for 30 minutes, or until golden brown.
erve warm with ice cream.

Serves 8

SPECIAL THANKS

A cookbook is a collaboration of many people.

To all those listed in this section, we thank you for your sponsorship, time, and effort on behalf of our project. We could not have succeeded without your dedication.

"The 1921 Seminole Theatre (built as a silent movie house by Homestead pioneers) utilized a Villager grant to replicate the original marquee in 1999."

THE VILLAGERS

Thank You

CULTURAL CONTRIBUTORS

The outpouring of support for this project has been overwhelming.
It has energized our group to know that so many support our cause.

Karen Alexander
Desiree Anthony
Martha V. Apolo
Renee J. Belair
Georgette F. Ballance
Joanna G. Barusch
Sheila W. Beebe
Ofelia Elena Beltran
Louise F. Bennett
Geri T. Berounsky
Cynthia Ann Bobson
Kathleen S. Bowker
Carol S. Brock
Carmen Ortiz-Butcher, M.D.
Alicia Callander
Debbie and Dennis Campbell
Ann Marie Clyatt
Coral Gables Garden Club
Coral Gables Woman's Club
Elisabeth D. Cozad
Dade County Farm Bureau
Diane Elaine Deen
Debby Ann Diaz
Charlotte C. Dison
Judy H. Dudek
Gayle S. Duncan
Marlin Ebbert
Alexis J. Ehrenhaft
Eileen "Sweet Pea" Ellman
Bob de la Fuente - J. R. Fry
Margie L. Gabriel
Toni D. Garcia
Jan P. Gardiner
Victoria Louise
Whitehurst-Glattfelder
Claire Angel
Whitehurst-Harris
James Convert Herrera

Linda Collins Hertz
Historical Museum of
Southern Florida
Verna R. Hodges
Eileen M. Hoffman
Sallye and Jim Jude
Susanne S. Kayyali
Irene V. Kogan
Penny E. Lambeth
Daru Sena Lane
Luz Norwood Le Baron
Maria "Connie" Lopez
Manya Lowman
Thane V. Malison
Kaye R. Martinez
Jo M. Mauk
Madeleine McIntosh
Maritza Martinez Mejia
Silvia A. Millor
Joan M. Mueller
Nannette "Nan" Neubauer
Norman Brothers
Produce, Inc.
Leslie S. Olle
Marjorie E. Palmer
Ana Rosa Phillips
Pinecrest Garden Club
Cathy Anne Prentice
Irene M. Priess
Margaret Pujals
Gayle Peters Pumo
Pauline "Polly" Ramos
Rodriguez and Quiroga
Architects
Anne Rosenstein
Marc D. Sarnoff,
City of Miami, Dist. 2
Karin G. Sastre

Sylvia Sheldon
Martha A. Stockhausen
Janet E. Stoker
Melody L. Swift
Kate B. Taylor
The Island Clinic at
Key Biscayne, LLC
The Kampong, N.T.B.G.
The Miami Woman's Club
The Woman's Club
of Coconut Grove
Jane W. Tinney – The Studio
Isabel M. Valdivia –
Chabela's Jewels
Sandra Kay Vanden
Mary "Jody" Verrengia
Lilian A. Walby
Anastasia "Stacy"
Webster-Briggle
Rosemary R. Welton
Lynn G. Wheeler
Leatrice and Al Damus
Karl and Dacia
Chaffin-Wiegandt
Maggie H. Wilson
Peggy M. Witt
Louan J. Zagarino
Linda Cooke Zahler
Dolores "Dee" Zell
Cathy Zuckerman
Coral Gables Chapter,
Daughters of the
American Revolution
Hirni's Wayside Garden Florist
Jody Crosland

STYLE & CONTENT CONSULTANTS

We could not have included the photographs of the historic properties and histories of our pioneers without each of the individuals and organizations giving of their time, facilities, and expertise.

Location Assistance

Adrienne Arsht

The Barnacle Historic State Park

Carrollton School of the Sacred Heart

David M. Brennan

Deering Estate at Cutler

Cindy L. Eckhart

The Honorable Margarita Esquiroz

Fairchild Tropical Botanic Garden

The Kampong of National
Tropical Botanical Garden

Victor Mendelson

Montgomery Botanical Center

Elaine and St. Julian Rosemond

The Honorable Scott J. Silverman

Ana M. Varela

Venetian Pool, City of Coral Gables

Virginia Key Beach Park Trust

Vizcaya Museum and Gardens

Photography

Robin Hill Photography, Inc.

Lulu & Petunia Photography, Inc.

Art Direction

Tom Reno Design
(Tom Reno, Hank McAfee, Dru Martin)

Pioneer Story Authors

Ray Allen

Dr. Paul George

Juanita Greene

Dr. Joel Hoffman

Carolyn Klepser

Bruce C. Matheson

Victor Mendelson

Hélène Muller Pancoast

Kit Pancoast Nagamura

Arva Moore Parks

Dr. Sandra Riley

Ellen J. Uguccioni

Printer

Scott Gamble, Printing Consultant

StorterChilds Printing Company, Inc.

RECIPE CONTRIBUTORS & TESTERS

A special thank you to our recipe contributors, who submitted their treasured recipes. Although we could not use them all, we certainly appreciate your generosity. And, to our dedicated testers, who conscientiously critiqued the recipes and gave useful feedback.

Contributors

Martha V. Apolo
The Barnacle State Park
Louise Bennett
Joan Gill Blank
Cindy Bobson
Kathleen Bowker
Kendra Brennan
Ann Marie Brennan
Charlene Butler
Lisa Wishart Chaffin
Lynn Chaffin
Pat Clarke
Malinda Cleary
Ann Marie Clyatt
Martha Anne Collins
Barbara Cook
Judy Dudek
Marlin Ebbert
Rafael Elias
Holly Evans
Marta Fernandez
Joe Fitzgerald
Linda Flores
Linda L. Flores
Margie Gabriel
Toni Garcia
Kay Gardner
Sunny Gates
Janet Green
Barbara Guilford
Mary Jo Hanson
Donna Hennessy
Kathy Herring
Linda Hertz
Verna Hodges
Eileen Hoffman

Jacqueline Huggett
Cindy Hutson
Carole Johnson
Bob and Sandy Jones
Lamar Kauffman
Kathleen Slesnick Kauffman
Susan Kay
Irene Krogan
Penny Lambeth
Daru Lane
Sarah Lane
Joan LaRoche
Luan LaRoche
Sherri Lee
Nancy Leslie
Lynn Lieberman
Anne Leidel
Thane Malison
Judy Mangasarian
Becky Roper Matkov
Jo Mauk
Madeleine McIntosh
City of Coral Gables, Merrick House
JoAnn Moebus
Anne Munday
Mimi Munroe
Meryl Nolan
Pat Ormond
Carmen Ortiz, MD
Hélène Muller Pancoast
Jane Allen Petrick, PhD
Barb Piper
Joyce Pipo
Judy Pruitt
Gayle Pumo
Edythe Quartin

Lynda Randolph
Anita L. Reeves
Colin Reeves
Amy Reyes
Carolyn Reyes
Ralph Reyes
Ivan Rodriguez
Madeline Rodriguez-Ortega
Bobbie Rosenberger
Tricia Sandler
Emily Savage
Joyce Seibert
Susan Shelley
Carol Stanfill
Martha Stockhausen
Eva Swift
Pamela Testerman
Mary Thelen
Holly Ebbert Troup
Ellen Uguccioni
Isabel M. Valdivia
Jeanette Van De Water
Sandy Vanden
Judy Verrengia
Judy Litwak
Jean Villanova
Caroline Weiss
Claire-Frances Flanagan- Whitehurst
Whole Foods Market
Maggie Wilson
Debbie Winter
Maxine B. Wishart
Peggy Witt
Mary Young
Amy Young
Scarlett Zachar

Louan Zagarino
Dottie Zinzow
Julie Ziska

Testers

Isabelle Andrews
Sheila Beebe
Vicky Belcher
Louisse Bennett
Renee Blair
Kathleen Bowker
Marlin Ebbert
Holly Evans
Janice Framke
Jody Gaché
Toni Garcia
Janet Green
Donna Hennessy
Janie Kinsella
Nina Korman
Thane Malison
Joan Mueller
Louise Petrine
Cathy Prentice
Judy Pruitt
Lynda Randolph
Sheila Revell
Barbie Steffen
Martha Stockhausen
Eva Swift
Isabel Valdivia
Jeanette Van De Water
Sandra Vanden
Jody Verrengia
Peggy Witt

Active

Pamela Jo Aarons
Karen Alexander
Elizabeth "Lisa" Guanci Allen
Desiree I. Anthony
Martha V. Apolo
Joanna Barusch
Sheila W. Beebe
Renée J. Belair
Louise F. Bennett
Kathleen S. Bowker
Kendra H. Brennan
Carol S. Brock
Lisa Wishart Chaffin
Lydia S. Clark
Ann Marie Clyatt
Martha Anne Collins
Debby Ann Diaz
Judy H. Dudek
Gayle S. Duncan
Alexis J. Ehrenhaft
Ann Eldredge
Sweet Pea Ellman
Holly B. Evans
Linda L. Flores
Margie L. Gabriel
Toni D. Garcia
Janet "Jan" P. Gardiner
Janet R. Green
Donna S. Hennessy
Clare R. M. Herrmann
Linda Collins Hertz
Verna R. Hodges
Carole Jean Johnson
Sallye G. Jude
Elizabeth "Liz" Juerling
Kathleen Slesnick Kauffman
Irene V. Kogan
Nina E. Korman
Barbara J. Lange
Silvia Licha
Manya Lowman
Thane Malison
Kaye R. Martinez
Madeleine McIntosh
Patricia G. Mederos
Brian Patrick Molloy
Joan M. Mueller
Carmen J. Ortiz
Marjorie E. Palmer
Irene Priess
Gayle Peters Pumo
Lynda Randolph
Anita Laura Reeves
Sheila W. Revell
Carolyn H. Reyes
Anne Rosenstein

Aloyma M. Sanchez Parissis
Norah Schaefer
Carol Stanfill
Eva A. Swift
Melody Swift
Joann Trombino
Kendell Turner
Isabel M. Valdivia
Sandra "Sandy" Vanden
Lilian A. Walby
Rosemary R. Welton
Lisa S. Wheeler
Lynn G. Wheeler
Claire-Frances Whitehurst
Maggie Hull Wilson
Maxine B. Wishart
Peggy Witt
Linda Cooke Zahler
Dolores "Dee" P. Zell
Cathy Zuckerman

Active New Members

Charles "Mike" M. Arnspiger
Jeanne Bunten
Mary E. Burke
Mary B. Deutsch
Helen M. Duncan
Stacy Eldredge
Nancy Terrell Elsas
Janet S. English
Monica Fitzgerald
Holly Freyre
Anita Friedlander
Renée M Garrett
Margaret "Peggy" Groves
Sallie Anne Jenks
Diane M. Lee
Suzanne Maule
Margaret McCaffery
Victoria M. Orr
Constance "Connie" Rico
Sharon Shelley-Taylor
Emma "Mimma" Tibaldeo
Julie Ziska

Active Life Members

Joan T. Bounds
Malinda Cleary
Eileen M. Hoffman
Frances "Dolly" MacIntyre
Pat Ormond
Pauline "Polly" Ramos
Ellen J. Uguccioni

Sustainers

Isabelle Andrews

Charlie Athos
Rita Ann Baker
Georgette Ballance
Joan Gill Blank
Cynthia Ann Bobson
April Bohatch
Patricia "Patti" Borcz
Phyllis Ann Borten
Ann T. Brody
Barbara S. Burdette
Christina Butler
Jan Case
Cynthia Christoph
Patricia "Pat" H. Clarke
Joni Armstrong Coffey
Margarita Courtney
Teresita E. de Blank
Diane Deen
Charlotte C. Dison
Anna L. Ehlert
Jacquelyn "Jackie" J. Esco
Marie Quinn Flanigan
Jo-Ann Forster
Janice Framke
Margaret L. Gaub
Lauren Harrison Genovese
Ghislaine Greene
Beryl Hamilton
Mary Jo Hanson
Shirley J. Harms
Shirley S. Harris
Elizabeth "Beth" Virginia Harrison
Jeanne Heyward
Jacqueline Huggett
Pamela Ibarguen
Susanne S. Kayyali
Diane Wallace Klemick
Penny Lambeth
Daru Lane
Aida Azcuy Lazzarin
Maria Conchita "Connie" Lopez
Ingrid D. Lyall
Elaine Lynn
Cynthia M. Lyons
Becky Roper Matkov
Jo M. Mauk
Candace McDonald
Silvia Millor
JoAnn C. Moebus
Joan H. Morris
Anne Munday
Ellen Clawson Nagel
Joyce E. Nelson
Luz Norwood-LeBaron
Leslie Olle
Nannette "Nan" Craver Neubauer
Ellen Winton

Oppenheimer
Betty Osborn
Lyn D'Alemberte Parks
Jane Allen Petrick
Ana Rosa Phillips
Cathy Anne Prentice
Judy Pruitt
Bonnie Prunka
Edythe J. Quartin
Rosa Maria Reeves
Bobbi Rosenberger
Stephanie Russell
Tricia Sandler
Joyce R. Seibert
Margaret Seroppian
Sylvia Sheldon
Susan G. Shelley
Rosemarie Stanford
Andrea Fay Stringos
Katherine "Kate" B. Taylor
Kitty Van Winkle Terry
Jane W. Tinney
Jaymes "Jaye" Turnbull
Marianne Ozok Vanevic
Bar Werner
Deborah Kathleen Winter
Harriet C. Wolf
Mary Martin Young
Louan Jones Zagarino

Sustainer Life Members

Vickie C. Belcher
Trish B. Bell
Geri Berounsky
Marianne "Mari" Brauzer
Elisabeth Cozad
Jody Crosland
Nina L. Derks
Marlin Ebbert
Marta N. Fernandez
Jody Gaché
Barbara F. Guilford
Doris Hartog
Margaret M. Kunz
Cheryl Newcomb Livesay
Judy White Mangasarian
Jane Noppenberg
Louise Petrine
Joyce P. Pippo
Karin G. Sastre
Martha Ann Stockhausen
Janet Elizabeth Stoker
"Cookie" Thelen
Jody Verrengia

INDEX

"A waterfall typical of the elegant landscape features found at Vizcaya Museum and Gardens."

APPETIZERS
*See also Dips;
Sandwiches; Spreads,
Cooking for a Crowd*

"Why I Fell In Love" Brie, 29
Bunuelos de Espinaca, 20
Cheesy Olive Puffs, 26
Chinese Chicken Sticks, 21
Crostini Primavera, 22
Ham and Cheese Crisps, 24
Hot and Spicy Chinese
   Shrimp, 25
Scallop Cebiche, 18
Spiced Nuts, 28
Spicy Almonds28,
Spicy Cayenne Toasts, 27
Yummy Hors d'Oeuvres, 25

APPLES
Apple Pecan Bread, 72
Baked Beans with Apples, 208
Caramelized Apple Tarts, 233
Chow-Chow, 90
Curried Tuna Salad, 69
Roasted Apples and
   Parsnips, 189
Sara's Paper Bag Pie, 226
Sister Jane's Easy Apple
   Cake, 215
Swedish Apple Cake, 220

ARTICHOKES
Artichoke Chicken Casserole, 145
Kay's Scalloped Tomatoes
   and Artichoke Hearts, 190

ASPARAGUS
Asparagus with Ginger-
   Orange Vinaigrette, 182
Farfalle with Mascarpone
   Asparagus, and Hazelnuts, 97
Swedish West Coast Seafood
   Salad, 54

AVOCADOS
Avocado Soup with Shrimp, 39
Stuffed Avocados with
   Creamed Lobster, 164
   Guacamole Dip, 23
Honeyed Pork Tenderloin
   with Avocado-Peach
   Salsa, 154
Roasted Pineapple and
   Avocado Salad, 63

BEANS
Baked Beans with Apples, 208
Black Bean Salad, 58
Black Bean Soup, 51
Georgia Caviar, 23
Kay's Black Bean & Papaya
   Salad, 202
Marta's Cuban Black Bean's, 183
Pasta Fagioli, 44
3 Bean Soup, 38
Tuscan Beef & Cannellini
   Stew, 143

BEEF
See also Stews

Corned Beef and Cabbage, 136
Fajitas, 140
Hearty Hodgepodge Soup, 199
Kay's Gypsy Soup, 45
Minced Beef Mix, 141
Oriental Meatloaf, 142
Steak à la Stroganoff, 137
Tenderloin with Green
   Peppercorn Sauce, 136

BISCUITS
Buttermilk Biscuits, 75

BREAD PUDDING
Mango Bread Pudding, 229
Pineapple Bread Pudding,
   214

BREADS
See also Muffins

Apple Pecan Bread, 72
Best Whole Wheat Banana
   Nut Bread, 74
Cheddar Corn Bread, 74
Cranberry Bread, 73
Harvest Bread, 77
Orange Bread, 79
Rum Banana Bread, 76
Sarah's Pumpkin Bread, 80
Strawberry Bread, 81
Tuscan Corn Bread, 85
Zucchini Bread, 83

BROWNIES
Swedish Brownies, 209

CAKE
Chocolate Chip Rum Cake, 216
Oatmeal Spice Cake, 217
Sherry Pound Cake, 219
Swedish Apple Cake, 220
Grandmother Bollin's Pound
   Cake, 216
Sister Jane's Easy Apple
   Cake, 215

CANNING TIPS
Canning Instructions, 91

CASSEROLES
See also Side Dishes

Artichoke Chicken
   Casserole, 145
Chicken Casserole, 205
Maxine's Turkey Casserole
   Supreme, 159
Shrimp Harpin, 176
Turkey and Wild Rice
   Casserole, 158

CHICKEN
See also Casseroles

Almond Crusted Chicken Salad, 56

Artichoke Chicken Casserole, 145

Auntie Janie's African Chicken, 146

Baked Chicken with Guava Sauce, 147

Chicken with Saffron, Green Olives and Mint, 149

Chinese Chicken Sticks, 21

Hattie's Southern Gumbo, 47

Indian Chicken, 148

Jerk Chicken Penne Pasta, 104

Lisa & Maxine's Chicken Salad, 200

Mango Chutney Chicken Salad, 67

Parmesan Crusted Chicken, 150

Party Chicken, 148

Rijstaffel Fairchild-Muller Curry with Condiments, 153

Shoppers Chicken, 144

Szechwan Chicken, 144

3 Bean Soup, 38

CHICKPEAS

Homemade Hummus, 19

Hummus with Tomatoes and Parsley, 19

Spaghetti with Chickpea Sauce, 102

COLLARD GREENS

Auntie Janie's Classic Collard Greens, 186

Collard Greens with Almonds, 186

CONDIMENTS

Chow-Chow, 90

Star Fruit Pickles, 87

Cranberry Chutney, 80

Green Mango Chutney 88

Spiced Cranberry Chutney, 89

Tomato Marmalade, 86

COOKIES

Bohemian Cookies, 230

Marlin's Gingersnaps, 222

Oatmeal Crispies, 215

Old Charleston Post Office Chewy Cake 219

Orange Slices Bar Cookies, 223

Potato Chip Cookies, 223

Ruby-Flecked Florentine Cookies, 221

CHOWDER

See also Soup, Gumbo

Charlie Frow's Chowder, 40

Queen Mabel's Chowder, 34

CHUTNEY

Cranberry Chutney, 80

Green Mango Chutney, 88

Spiced Cranberry Chutney, 89

CRAB

Becky's Deviled Crab, 169

Crab and Sweet Potato Soup, 43

Hattie's Southern Gumbo, 47

Joan Gill Blank's Fabulous Fish Soup, 36

Seafood Cakes, 174

CUSTARDS/ PUDDINGS

Cuban Flan, 231

Lemon Mousse with Berry Puree, 225

Mango Bread Pudding 229

Pineapple Bread Pudding, 214

COOKING FOR A CROWD

Baked Beans with Apples 208

Caponata Dip, 198

Chicken Casserole, 205

Cranberry Jell-O, 203

Frogmore Stew, 205

Hash Brown Potato Casserole, 209

Hearty Hodgepodge Soup, 199

Italian Strata, 196

Kay's Black Bean and Papaya Salad, 202

Leg of Lamb with Roasted Tomato-Olive Sauce, 207

Lime-Pear Jell-O Salad, 203

Lisa and Maxine's Chicken Salad, 200

Mariner's Rum Punch, 210

Oscar's Champagne Punch, 211

Pita Cheese Crisps, 197

Smoked Fish Dip, 197

Snappy Bites, 198

Spinach Strata, 206

Strawberry Tea, 211

Swedish Brownies, 209

The Barnacle's Brandy Punch, 210

Tortellini Salad, 201

Tropical Buffalo Wings, 196

Warm Ham and Cheese Sandwiches, 204

DESSERTS
See also Cakes; Cookies; Custards/Puddings; Pies/Tarts

"Why I Fell In Love" Brie, 29

Blueberry Crisp, 228

Mini "Watermelon" Wedges, 224

Orange Float, 232

Peach Cobbler, 229

Pumpkin Squares, 218

Strawberry Sorbet, 214

DESSERTS
(Continued)

Swedish Brownies, 209

Wendy's Pavlova, 227

DIPS

Georgia Caviar, 23

Guacamole Dip, 23

Homemade Hummus, 19

Hummus with Tomatoes and Parsley, 19

DRINKS

The Barnacle's Brandy Punch, 210

Blueberry Vodka, 31

Carmella's Kahlua, 30

Mango Margaritas 31

Mariner's Rum Punch, 210

Oscar's Champagne Punch, 211

Spiced Chilled Wine, 30

Strawberry Tea, 211

DUCK

Nutty Duck Breast Salad, 65

Rijstaffel Fairchild-Muller Curry with Condiments, 153

GRANOLA

Cookie's Homemade Granola, 84

GRITS

Easy Garlic Shrimp and Grits, 166

GUMBO

Hattie's Southern Gumbo, 47

JAM

Mother Hanson's Mango Jam, 90

Tomato Marmalade, 86

LAMB

Leg of Lamb with Roasted Tomato-Olive Sauce, 207

Rijstaffel Fairchild-Muller Curry with Condiments, 153

LOBSTER

Stuffed Avocados with Creamed Lobster, 164

Joan Gill Blank's Fabulous Fish Soup, 36

Madeleine's Lobster Thermidor, 163

KIELBASA

Frogmore Stew, 205

Yummy Hors d'Oeuvres, 25

MANGOES

Green Mango Chutney, 88

Mango Margaritas, 31

Mother Hanson's Mango Jam, 90

Papaya-Mango Salsa, 178

Thai-Style Pumpkin Soup, 49

Warm Mango Bread Pudding, 229

MAIN COURSE SALADS
See also Salads

Almond Crusted Chicken Salad, 56

Curried Tuna Salad, 69

Lisa and Maxine's Chicken Salad, 200

Mango Chutney Chicken, 67

Nutty Duck Breast Salad, 65

Salmon Niçoise, 66

Swedish West Coast Seafood Salad, 54

MARINADE

Jerk Marinade, 104

Orange Dijon, 175

MUFFINS

Bran Muffins, 73

Dill Mini Muffins, 78

Great Dried Fruit Muffins, 76

NUTS

Spiced Nuts, 28

Spicy Almonds, 28

ORANGES

Orange Bread, 79

Orange Dijon Salmon, 175

Orange Teriyaki Honey Dressing, 56

Orange Float, 232

PAPAYA

Green Mango Chutney, 88

Hawaiian Pork Patties with Pineapple-Papaya Sauce, 139

Kay's Black Bean and Papaya Salad, 202

Papaya-Mango Salsa, 178

PASTA

Black Mussels with Linguini, 101

Broccoli Pasta with Two Cheeses, 99

Farfalle with Mascarpone, Asparagus, and Hazelnuts, 97

Fluted Shells with Spicy Carrot Sauce, 103

Jack's Baked Ziti, 96

Jerk Chicken Penne Pasta, 104

Manicotti, 99

Norcina, 106

Penne with Vodka Cream Sauce, 107

Scallop Pasta with Saffron Sauce, 96

Shrimp Cacciatore with Penne Pasta, 98

Spaghetti Carbonara, 105

Spaghetti with Chickpea Sauce, 102

Summer Linguini with Tomatoes and Basil, 100

PICKLES

Star Fruit Pickles, 87

PIES/TARTS

Banana Split Pie, 228

Caramelized Apple Tarts, 233

Key Lime Pie, 220

No-Bake Key Lime Pie, 222

Praline Pumpkin Pie, 230

Sara's Paper Bag Pie, 226

Square Mousse Pie, 218

PINEAPPLE

Roasted Pineapple and Avocado Salad, 63

Hawaiian Pork Patties with Pineapple-Papaya Sauce, 139

Pineapple Bread Pudding, 214

Scarlett's Acorn Squash, 188

PORK

Hawaiian Pork Patties with Pineapple-Papaya Sauce, 139

Honeyed Pork Tenderloin with Avocado-Peach Salsa, 154

Pork Fried Rice, 155

Sauerkraut and Ribs, 155

Spicy Pork Tenderloin, 156

Tonkatsu, 157

POTATOES

Boston Style Potato Pancakes, 193

Ellen's "Au Rotten" Potatoes, 187

Hash Brown Potato Casserole, 209

Portuguese Mashed Potatoes, 192

RELISH

Chow-Chow, 90

QUICHE

Zucchini Pie, 152

Broccoli Cheese Quiche, 151

RICE

Apricot Rice, 189

Coronado Brown Rice Casserole, 184

Lemon Rice, 182

Pork Fried Rice, 155

Turkey and Wild Rice Casserole, 158

SALAD DRESSING

Ginger Lime Vinaigrette 202

Toni's Vinaigrette, 55

Homemade Caesar, 68

Lemon Dressing, 66

Mango Chutney Dressing, 64

Orange Teriyaki Honey Dressing, 56

Poppy Seed Dressing, 62

Raspberry Vinaigrette, 57

Rhode Island Sauce, 55

Ginger Lime Vinaigrette, 202

Homemade Caesar, 68

Lemon Dressing, 66

Mango Chutney, 64

Orange Teriyaki Honey Dressing, 56

Poppy Seed Dressing, 62

Raspberry Vinaigrette, 57

Rhode Island Sauce, 55

Toni's Vinaigrette, 55

SALADS

See also Main Course Salads

Amy's Salad, 59

Black Bean Salad, 58

Broccoli Salad, 59

Cranberry Jell-O, 203

Curried Spinach Salad, 64

Endive Salad with Pear and Walnuts, 57

Green Bean, Beet, and Feta Salad, 68

Jacqueline's Strawberry Spinach Salad, 62

Kay's Black Bean and Papaya Salad, 202

Lime-Pear Jell-O Salad, 203

Roasted Pineapple and Avocado Salad, 63

Sweet and Sour Asian Cucumbers, 60

Tortellini Salad, 201

Watermelon and Arugula Salad, 61

Wishart Family Herbed Tomatoes, 60

SALMON

Baked Salmon with Dill Sauce, 170

Barbeque Roasted Salmon, 167

Garlic Salmon, 168

Orange Dijon Salmon, 175

Salmon Niçoise, 66

Salmon Party Ball, 18

SALSA

Avocado-Peach Salsa, 154

Papaya-Mango Salsa, 178

SANDWICHES

Tea Sandwiches from the Savoy, London, 82

Villager Tea Sandwiches, 92

Warm Ham and Cheese Sandwiches, 204

SAUCES

Balsamic Vinegar Butter Sauce, 150

Cheese Wine Sauce, 175

Chickpea Sauce, 103

Chile-Ginger Sauce, 168

Chimichurri Sauce, 152

Daru's Meuniere Sauce, 171

Dill Sauce, 170

Fresh Tomato, 165

Garlic-Cilantro Dressing, 174

Ginger Soy Dressing, 162

Green Peppercorn Sauce, 136

Guava Sauce, 147

Miso Sauce, 166

Pineapple-Papaya Sauce, 139

Roasted Tomato-Olive Sauce, 207

Saffron Sauce, 96

Spicy Carrot Sauce, 103

Sweet and Sour Sauce, 21

Tomato Sauce for Fish Soup, 36

Tonkatsu Sauce, 157

Vodka Cream Sauce, 107

SCALLOPS

Joan Gill Blank's Fabulous Fish Soup, 36

Scallop Cebiche, 18

Scallop Pasta with Saffron Sauce, 96

Scallop Stew, 179

SEAFOOD

Stuffed Avocados with Creamed Lobster, 164

Baked Fish Filets with a

Fresh Tomato Sauce, 165

Baked Salmon with Dill Sauce, 170

Baked Sea Bass in Miso Sauce, 166

Barbeque Roasted Salmon, 167

Becky's Deviled Crab, 169

Black Mussels with inguini, 101

Camarones Al Ajillo, 177

Chile-Ginger Sauce, 168

Daru's Meuniere Sauce, 171

Easy Garlic Shrimp and Grits, 166

Garlic Salmon, 168

Joan Gill Blank's Fabulous Fish Soup, 36

Judy's Sea Bass, 173

Madeleine's Lobster Thermidor, 163

Orange Dijon Salmon, 175

Papaya-Mango Salsa, 178

Queen Mabel's Chowder, 34

Scallop Stew, 179

Seafood Cakes, 174

Seared Sesame Tuna with Ginger and Garlic, 162

Shrimp Harpin, 176

Shrimp Moutarde, 177

Snapper Française, 172

Snapper in a Cheese Wine Sauce, 175

SHRIMP

Avocado Soup with Shrimp, 39

Cold Shrimp Soup, 43

Easy Garlic Shrimp and Grits, 166

Hot and Spicy Chinese Shrimp, 25

Seafood Cakes, 174

Shrimp Harpin, 176

Shrimp in Garlic Sauce, 177

Shrimp Moutarde, 177

Swedish West Coast Seafood Salad, 54

SIDE DISHES

Apricot Rice, 189

Asparagus with Ginger-Orange Vinaigrette, 182

Baked Beans with Apples, 208

Boston Style Potato Pancakes193

Carrots with Horseradish Glaze, 184

Cauliflower-Tomato Au Gratin, 185

Collard Greens with Almonds, 186

Coronado Brown Rice Casserole, 184

Ellen's "Au Rotten" Potatoes, 187

Hash Brown Potato Casserole, 209

Hungarian Noodles, 188

Jalapeno Corn Casserole, 185

Kay's Scalloped Tomatoes and Artichoke Hearts, 190

Lemon Rice, 182

Marta's Cuban Black Bean's, 183

Portuguese Mashed Potatoes 192

Roasted Apples and Parsnips, 189

Sautéed Baby Bok Choy, 190

Scarlett's Acorn Squash, 188

Whole Roasted Cauliflower with Lemon Caper Dressing, 191

SOUP

See also Chowder, Gumbo

Avocado Soup with Shrimp, 39

Black Bean Soup, 51

Butternut Squash Parsnip Soup, 41

Cold Cucumber Soup, 42

Cold Shrimp Soup, 43

Crab and Sweet Potato Soup, 43

Gazpacho, 44

Hearty Hodgepodge Soup, 199

Joan Gill Blank's Fabulous Fish Soup, 36

Kay's Gypsy Soup, 45

Lentil Soup, 48

Mushroom Soup, 46

Pasta Fagioli, 44

Potage of Turnips Leeks and Potatoes, 50

Thai-Style Pumpkin Soup, 49

3 Bean Soup, 38

SPREADS

Deviled Ham, 26

Homemade Hummus, 19

Hummus with Tomatoes and Parsley, 19

Salmon Party Ball, 18

Sun-Dried Tomato Spread, 27

Sweet Onion Spread, 20

STEWS

Scallop Stew, 179

Tuscan Beef & Cannellini Stew, 143

Frogmore Stew, 205

SUPPER RECIPES

Artichoke Chicken Casserole, 145

Auntie Janie's African Chicken, 146

Baked Chicken with Guava Sauce, 147

Beef Filet's with Green Peppercorn Sauce, 136

Broccoli Cheese Quiche, 151

Chicken with Saffron, Green Olives and Mint, 149

Corned Beef and Cabbage, 138

Fajitas, 140

Hawaiian Pork Patties with Pineapple-Papaya Sauce, 139

Honeyed Pork Tenderloin with Avocado-Peach Salsa, 154

Indian Chicken, 148

Maxine's Turkey Casserole Supreme, 158

Minced Beef Mix, 141

Oriental Meatloaf, 142

Parmesan Crusted Chicken, 150

Party Chicken, 148

Pork Fried Rice, 155

Rijstaffel Fairchild-Muller Curry with Condiments, 153

Leg of Lamb with Roasted Tomato-Olive Sauce, 207

Sauerkraut and Ribs, 155

Shoppers Chicken, 144

Spicy Pork Tenderloin, 156

Steak à la Stroganoff, 137

Szechwan Chicken, 144

Tenderloin with Green Peppercorn Sauce, 136

Tonkatsu, 157

Turkey and Wild Rice Casserole, 158

Zucchini Pie, 152

TOMATOES

Avocado-Peach Salsa, 154

Baked Salmon with Dill Sauce, 170

Black Bean Salad, 58

Caponata Dip, 198

Cauliflower-Tomato Au Gratin, 185

Crostini Primavera, 22

Fajitas, 140

Joan Gill Blank's Fabulous Fish Soup, 36

Kay's Scalloped Tomatoes and Artichoke Hearts, 190

Roasted Tomato-Olive Sauce, 207

Salmon Niçoise Salad, 66

Spicy Cayenne Toasts with Sun Dried Tomato Spread, 27

Summer Linguini with Tomato and Basil, 100

Swedish West Coast Seafood Salad, 54

Tomato Marmalade, 86

Tortellini Salad, 201

Wishart Family Herbed Tomatoes, 60

TURKEY

Maxine's Turkey Casserole Supreme, 159

Rijstaffel Fairchild-Muller Curry with Condiments, 153

Turkey and Wild Rice Casserole, 158

VEGETABLES
See also Casseroles

Asparagus with Ginger-Orange Vinaigrette, 182

Carrots with Horseradish Glaze, 184

Cauliflower-Tomato Au Gratin, 185

Collard Greens with Almonds, 186

Jalapeno Corn Casserole, 185

Kay's Scalloped Tomatoes and Artichoke Hearts, 190

Roasted Apples and Parsnips, 189

Sautéed Baby Bok Choy, 190

Scarlett's Acorn Squash, 188

Whole Roasted Cauliflower with Lemon Caper Dressing, 191

Wishart Family Herbed Tomatoes, 60

THE VILLAGERS

INCORPORATED

DEDICATED TO THE RESTORATION AND PRESERVATION OF HISTORIC SITES